NAVAJO AGING

NAVAJO AGING

▶▶▶ ◀◀◀

THE TRANSITION FROM FAMILY
TO INSTITUTIONAL SUPPORT

Stephen J. Kunitz
Jerrold E. Levy

With
Tracy Andrews, Donald Callaway, Chena DuPuy,
Eric Henderson, and Dennis Parker

Photographs by
Jonathan L. Bayer

THE UNIVERSITY OF ARIZONA PRESS / TUCSON

96   95   94   93   92   91   6   5   4   3   2   1

Library of Congress Cataloging-in-Publication Data

Kunitz, Stephen J.
    Navajo aging: the transition from family to institutional support / Stephen J. Kunitz
and Jerrold E. Levy with Tracy Andrews . . . [et al.] ; photographs by Jonathan L.
Bayer.
        p.   cm.
    Includes bibliographical references and index.
    ISBN 0-8165-1260-4
    1. Navajo Indians—Aged—Health and hygiene. I. Levy, Jerrold E., 1930–
II. Bayer, Jonathan, 1936– . III. Title.
RA448.5.I5K86 1991
362.1'9897--dc20   91-3178
                                                                              CIP

British Library Cataloguing in Publication data are available.

Part of chapter 5 of this book was originally published in the journal *Culture, Medicine,
and Society* 10 (1986): 97–122, and is reprinted by permission of Kluwer Academic Pub-
lishers. Part of chapter 6 was originally published in *The Journal of Cross-Cultural Gerontology* 3 (1988): 71–85, and is reprinted by permission of the journal. Parts of this book
were also originally published in an essay in *Aging and Health: Perspectives on Gender, Race,
Ethnicity, and Class,* edited by Kyriakos S. Markides, pp. 211–245, copyright © 1989 by
Sage Publications, and are reprinted by permission of Sage Publications, Inc.

The research on which this book is based was supported by a grant (RO1 AG03403)
from the National Institute on Aging.

CONTENTS

Figures

TABLES

►► 1 ◄◄

INTRODUCTION

THE AGING OF Western industrial populations is generally thought to be a direct consequence of the industrial revolution, which improved living conditions, thereby lowering birth and death rates and converting the most prevalent diseases from infectious to man-made and degenerative. It is also commonly thought that as part of the same process the status of the aged has declined due to the decreased importance of agricultural land as a source of status, the decreased importance of the multigenerational extended family, increased geographic mobility, and rapidly changing technology (Cowgill 1972; Palmore and Manton 1974).

That the impact of these changes on the elderly is often seen in a negative light is not surprising when one recalls that the social sciences are largely a product of the concerns generated by the transformation of European society in the course of the nineteenth century from one based largely on agriculture to one based largely on industry. The impact on communities, families, and individuals has been the source of some of the most fruitful insights of social philosophers. Although many of the writers most often cited as the fathers of social science agreed that the industrial and democratic revolutions had freed individuals from the constraints as well as the supports of church, kin, and community, they were by no means exhilarated by these changes. Indeed, many of them were at least ambivalent if not deeply conservative in their idealization of the face-to-face community, the established hierarchy of the old order, and the sense of permanence engendered by the eternal seasonal cycles to which the rural dweller was so attuned (Nisbet 1966).

This complex of changes—from rural to urban life, from agriculture to industry, from extended to neolocal family organization, from high to low fertility and mortality, from nonliterate to literate, from *gemeinschaft* to *gesellschaft*—has often been subsumed under the rubric of *modernization*. It is an ambiguous term, for it carries with it such negative connotations as alienation, anomie, and social isolation, as well as such positive connotations as an active rather than a passive view of life and a sense of mastery rather than of fatalism. Many social scientists no longer find modernization a useful notion, for the uniform processes once assumed to be involved have been found instead to be diverse and highly variable.

Nonetheless, in the field of social epidemiology, which is concerned with the health effects of social institutions and social change, the underlying assumption has generally been that social change results in untoward consequences. This assumption is derived largely from the influence of John Cassel, who deserves credit as the intellectual progenitor of the field. His work in turn drew heavily upon that of the social scientists who were most dominant through the 1950s, among whom ideas of the disruptive effects of social change were often especially clear (Cassel et al. 1960). Cassel was particularly impressed by the many observations that indicated that culture change led to the disruption of traditional ties that bound people to their kin and communities and that such disruption was often followed by disease and even death. Indeed, a number of prospective studies of social support and subsequent health published in recent years report an inverse relationship between social support and mortality either in the general population (Berkman and Syme 1979; House et al. 1982) or among the elderly (Blazer 1982; Zuckerman et al. 1984). Studies examining the effects of social support on morbidity, pregnancy outcomes, and mother-infant interactions (Berkman 1984) have reached similar conclusions. Most of the work on social relations and health services deals with the utilization of hospitals, doctors, and dentists, as well as compliance with professionals' recommendations (Cobb 1976; Geertsen et al. 1975; Kunitz and Tsianco 1981; McKinlay 1973; Suchman 1964, 1965).

The social changes that have often been assumed to be part of the modernization process—the disruption of traditional bonds of kinship and community—have not invariably led to either a deterioration of the status of the elderly (Foner 1984) or to worsening health. In some situations, high unemployment has meant that control by the elderly of scarce agricultural land enhances their status. In other groups, the availability of government pensions has made elderly people the major source of cash so that it is in the interests of the young to keep them alive. Among the Western Apaches, according to Goodwin (1969:512–517), the result of government pensions was that the elderly received better care than they had before pensions became available. Much depends on the kind of society that had previously existed and the context within which the process occurs, whether a newly independent nation, a large welfare state in which tribal minorities live in more or less isolated enclaves, a society with full employment, or one with a high rate of unemployment.

Studies of health consequences of social change have produced conflicting results. Here we do not discuss the unprecedented low mortality achieved by many peoples in the twentieth century and consider only the noninfectious diseases that are now most common in Europe, the Americas, and much of Asia. For example, a prospective study of the consequences of North Sea oil development on the physical and mental health of Shetland Islanders discovered that people in the impact area fared better than people in a control area protected from the development. When significant financial benefits were realized, health improved. A combination of negative life events and financial strain among people in the protected area seemed to be most predictive of poor health (Suzman et al. 1980). On the other hand, studies of South Sea Islanders who migrated to New Zealand show an increasing incidence of hypertension compared to those who remained at home (Salmond et al. 1989).

The reason, then, that the idea of modernization is no longer used by many social scientists is that it is not one process. The social changes it has been assumed to embody are not invariably predictive of an enhanced or diminished status for the elderly or of improved or worsening health. On the other hand, a tradition of research suggests that the transformation of kin-based societies under the impact of forces emanating from Euro-American societies—education, rural to urban migration, factory rather than agricultural work, and the expropriation of resources—has resulted in demoralization, poor health, and an increase in social pathologies such as alcoholism, child and elder abuse, homicide, and suicide. This tradition has informed both social epidemiology and most of the work among American Indians, and it forms the background of the present study.

In this study of the relationship between health status, health care utilization, and the family organization of a sample of elderly Navajos, we pay special attention to the question of whether social support or the lack thereof has a measurable influence on health status. As young adults in the 1930s, the subjects of our research experienced the destruction of a traditional pastoral economy that had persisted from the beginning of the nineteenth century until the stock reduction programs of the 1930s and 1940s. They are also the first generation reared almost entirely in a traditional health culture to have the option of using a comprehensive, modern health delivery system provided by the federal government. The economic transformation worked by the stock reduction programs eroded but did not completely destroy the cooperating kin networks of the pastoral economy. The stresses of adaptation to a new way of life experienced by this generation of Navajos may well have had an influence on their health, mortality, and utilization of modern health services. If contact with kin is conducive to good health, then those elderly Navajos still living in extended families ought to be in better health than those who are most isolated. Alternatively, in kin-based societies, especially under conditions of poverty, contact with kin by the elderly is likely to be virtually universal and may be either exploitative or beneficial. If this is the case among the Navajo, we might expect to find no relationship or even an inverse one between contact with kin and health. In fact, we have found very little association between social isolation and poor health. Before proceeding, however, we shall describe social and economic conditions on the Navajo Reservation, particularly in the area where we worked.

The Setting

Since 1868, when the Navajos returned to their treaty reservation straddling what was to become the Arizona–New Mexico border, the reservation has been enlarged until it now encompasses about 24,000 square miles in northeastern and north central Arizona, northwestern New Mexico, and southeastern and south central Utah.

Although the reservation is bordered by the San Juan and Colorado rivers on the north and west and is cut by the Little Colorado River in the southwest, relatively little of the water from these rivers has been available to the Navajos for agricultural or industrial purposes (Reno 1981). Mineral resources, however, include coal, oil, uranium, and copper, most of it found in the eastern end, where much extraction has occurred since the 1920s (Kelly 1968; Parman 1976). A large coalfield on Black Mesa in the central portion of the reservation has been strip mined since the 1970s. Copper and uranium were formerly mined in the western part of the reservation but are no longer. The fact that natural resources are most concentrated on and adjacent to the eastern end of the reservation explains the greater concentration of border towns and non-Indians in that area, as well as the greater population density.

The richness of mineral resources, the poverty of agriculture, bureaucratic impediments, and institutional policies have combined to create what is sometime termed a dual economy (Levy 1980; Reno 1981; for a slightly different view, see Wood 1980). Heavily capitalized non-Navajo enterprises have dominated the extraction of non-renewable resources while failing to provide significant employment.

With employment low and subsistence and commercial livestock raising and agriculture unproductive, the Navajo economy is kept afloat by employment in federal, tribal, and state organizations providing health and human services, by a variety of sources of welfare support, and by off-reservation wage work (Kunitz 1983). In this context, the traditional form of extended family organization has continued to be adaptive because manpower must be deployed not only to accomplish many necessary domestic chores, such as sheepherding and hauling wood and water, but also to take advantage of whatever occasional employment becomes available. The sharing of vehicles and sources of income, whether earned or unearned (Supplemental Security Income and Aid to Dependent Children, for example), is a major function of this form of family organization (Henderson 1979; Aberle 1981).

Differences in the availability of natural resources and access to border towns are reflected in regional differences in income, educational levels, and dependence on wage work and welfare across the reservation. In general, the eastern end is characterized by greater involvement in the wage economy, and the western end by greater dependence on welfare (Kunitz 1977a, 1977b, 1983). Demographically, too, there are significant differences. Population growth has been more rapid in the east than the west despite higher mortality rates

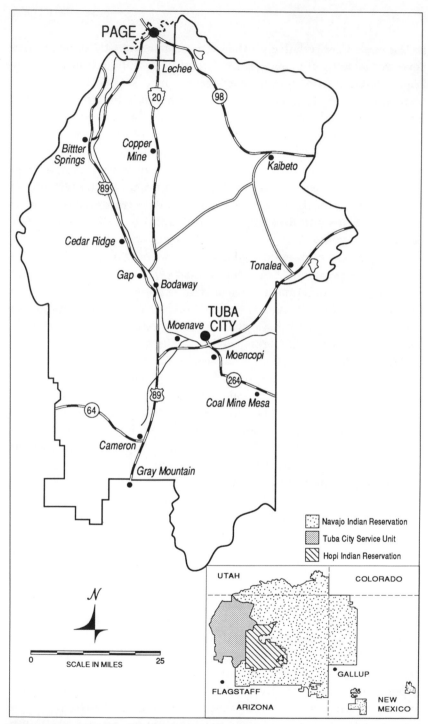

Figure 1.1. The Tuba City Service Unit

in the east. Fertility does not show the clear regional differences it once did. Instead, the more rapid population growth in the east is due to migration to sources of wage work.

Despite these differences, it does not seem that the age structure of the population differs dramatically by region. So far as we have been able to estimate from the 1980 census, in which a considerable amount of underreporting seems to have occurred, the age distribution is approximately as follows: 0–18 years, 50 percent; 19–64 years, 45 percent; and 65 and above, 5 percent. At the community level, however, there are differences: wage work settlements tend to have younger populations than rural areas.

Our fieldwork was done in the Tuba City Service Unit, a catchment area designated by the Indian Health Service of the U.S. Public Health Service as being served by the hospital and field programs of the Tuba City Indian Hospital on the westernmost part of the reservation. This area includes Upper and Lower Sonoran life zones characterized by desert grassland and scrub as well as piñon and juniper at higher elevations (Figure 1.1).

There were some Navajos, Paiutes, and Hopis in this area before the reservation period began, but intensive settlement by Navajos seems not to have begun much before the 1880s. These early Navajo settlers lived in widely dispersed camps that even as late as the 1930s controlled larger flocks and more land than camps in the east, where settlement was more dense. Since then, of course, the land has become more thickly settled as population has grown both by natural increase and immigration. Even now, however, population density is lower than in the east. Although there are fewer wage-work opportunities, the full range of Navajo communities is found, from isolated rural areas to new settlements adjacent to a coal-fired electrical generating station and to Tuba City, the administrative and service center of the western Navajo. In the years since our first fieldwork in the late 1950s, Tuba City has grown from perhaps 1,000 to almost 10,000 people. A variety of tribal and government housing projects have been built. There is now a supermarket, several motels, a car dealership, two movie theaters, a new 125-bed hospital, and a large school complex.

In the early 1970s, strip mining began on Black Mesa (in District 4), and some of the coal was transported to a new power plant near Page, Arizona, which had been created in the 1960s as the base of the construction operations of the then-new Glen Canyon Dam. Many Navajos came to work at the construction site of the new generating station, located at the northern boundary of District 1. Other areas remained largely untouched by these developments, however. A series of surveys in several communities at that time provides evidence of the diversity to be found in our study area (Callaway et al. 1976).

The settlements surveyed included Red Lake (a rural area), Tuba City, and the region near the site of the new power plant that consisted of several distinct settlements, some that were composed entirely of male construction workers living in motels and dormitories, and others that included families. Households in the wage-work settlements were younger, smaller, and better educated than those in Red Lake and Tuba City. Male household heads in Red Lake had an average of 4.7 years of schooling; in Tuba City, 7.3; and in the new areas, between 5.9 and 10.8. The average age of male household heads in Red Lake was 47.8 years; in Tuba City, 42.2; and in the new areas, between 28.8 and 38.6. There were hardly any female heads of households in the new wage-work areas. Average ages in Red Lake and Tuba City were 52.7 and 46.8 years, respectively. In rural Red Lake, 64 percent were widowed and 36 percent divorced.

Per capita income was remarkably low in all three areas, with the lowest ($895) reported for rural Red Lake and the highest ($3,121) in one of the new wage-work settlements. Despite the high proportion of income derived from wage work in the new settlements (86–90 percent) all groups still owned livestock, both for income and for domestic consumption. This was not a significant source of support in any group, however, providing only 5 percent of total income in Red Lake and between 1 and 2 percent in all other areas. Unearned income was higher in the groups with low wage income than in the wage-work population. Thus, while income was low among all groups, the sources differed. The most rural group was dependent almost equally on wage work and welfare—50 and 40 percent, respectively. As wage work increased, dependence on welfare and livestock both declined.

Although households tended to be smaller in the new settlements—four persons, as opposed to more than six in Tuba City and Red Lake—this may simply have been a function of the relative youth of the household heads and their spouses in this area. In all areas, however, single-family households predominated, nowhere being less than 60 percent.

Navajos are said to have traditionally lived in multihousehold settlements called camps. A matrilocal postnuptial residence rule leads to the formation of matrilocal extended families composed of a parent couple, their unmarried offspring, and their married daughters with their spouses and children. With the exception of one small community, the new settlements averaged only one household per camp and had a higher proportion of camps containing a single household. Single-household camps, however, were the most common camp type everywhere, totaling 78 and 70 percent in Red Lake and Tuba City. In another rural community, on Black Mesa in District 4, which was surveyed at the same time, only 36 percent of camps were composed of single households. Thus there may be as much or more variation among rural settlements as there is between urban and rural.

Although the matrilocal camp is still the dominant form of extended family, the large proportion of single-household camps raises the question of whether the extended family has declined as the level of wage work has increased. In all areas of the reservation, the proportion of income derived from wage work and unearned income, primarily welfare, has increased steadily while that from farming, craft production, and stock raising has declined. Yet it is not at all clear that the proportion of neolocal, single-household families has increased as well. In 1940 the Human Dependency Surveys showed that some 53 percent of all Navajo consumption units (camps) were single-family households (Henderson and Levy 1975).

In a poor population such as this, involvement in wage work and increased educational attainment do not necessarily mean that family organization changes markedly. Indeed, dependence on unstable sources of income, which is characteristic of the construction workers in the new settlements as well as of many other wage workers, may encourage dependence on kin. At the same time, in the three areas we have described, single families are the most common form of household, and independent households are the most common type of camp. It is also true, however, that rural poverty does encourage young people to seek wage work in administrative centers like Tuba City, in new settlements, and off the reservation. Thus there seems to be a drain of young people from rural areas, and we may expect that while the age structure of the total population will continue to be young for some years to come, residual populations of the elderly are likely to develop in many places where employment is unavailable and where pastoralism has long since ceased to be economically viable.

THE RESEARCH

Like many Third World countries, the Navajos received the benefits of modern medical care without the modernization of their economy, and the demographic transition was effected more by medical technology than by a great improvement in living conditions. In consequence, the relationship between social support and health status among the Navajo may be quite different from that found by studies of the general population. In industrialized societies it is likely that large, coresident families are most often formed by choice rather than necessity. They may, in consequence, be more truly supportive than those found in a population like that of the Navajo where sources of income are unstable and where income and labor must be pooled to ensure survival.

To test the notion that social support has a positive effect on health and hospital utilization, we conducted a survey of elderly Navajos living in the Tuba City Service Unit. The study sample consisted of 278 people who in 1982 were 65 years of age or older. Individuals were chosen at random from a computer-generated list of all people born in 1917 or earlier who had been treated at least once in an Indian Health Service clinic or hospital in the previous ten years and who had given an address within the Tuba City Service Unit, the catchment area of approximately 5,000 square miles forming the universe to which we limited our attention. Eight people (3 percent) refused to be interviewed. The final sample was 270.

It is conceivable that by choosing the sample in this way we did not include people who had never had any contact with the Public Health Service system of medical care, by far the most significant source of services (free of charge to Indian beneficiaries) on the reservation. This is unlikely to have led to significant ascertainment bias, however, since it seems improbable that a substantial proportion of the population would not have had contact with a health care provider at least once in ten years. Moreover, comparing the size of the population as estimated by our method with the number enumerated by the 1980 census indicates that the census missed about 15 percent of the people aged 65 and above in this region. The people we interviewed were a 50 percent random sample of all the people on the initial list who had not died or moved away and whose place of residence was accurately given as within the service unit.

Two sources of data were used. One was an extensive interview, usually lasting three to four hours and most often carried out in

Navajo, which gathered data on (a) family organization and economics; (b) the level of physical, social, and intellectual functioning (the Sickness Impact Profile; see Gilson et al. 1975; Bergner et al. 1976a, 1976b; Pollard et al. 1976); and (c) a series of questions related to depression and personal characteristics. The second source of data consisted of a review (with the respondent's consent) of inpatient and outpatient medical records. Only one respondent refused permission for this review. Data collected from the records included diagnoses, number and duration of hospitalizations (including those in hospitals elsewhere, on- or off-reservation, when known), and all surgical procedures and diagnostic tests. Verbatim transcriptions were made of all references to, or diagnoses of, any psychiatric or cognitive disorder including depression. The details of sampling and interviewing are given in appendix 1. The dependent and independent variables are described in detail in chapter 3. Suffice it to say here that the independent variables were designed to tap various dimensions of social organization, economic status and sources of income, and religious knowledge and participation, all of which previous investigators have found to be related to health status.

Measures of family size, frequency of visits by relatives, and the like at a given moment tell little about the quality of family interaction. Nor can synchronous surveys tell us much about historical trends or people's reactions to them. We have attempted to rectify this in chapter 2 by presenting a history of one large kin group from the days before stock reduction to the present. We had worked with these related families since 1959 and were able to reconstruct much of their economic, social, religious, and medical histories from our field notes. For earlier years we have relied on the history and genealogical material gathered by Henderson (1985) in his study of the northern portion of the Tuba City Service Unit.

In chapter 3, patterns of hospital utilization and their relation to self-reported levels of function are examined. The self-reported measures of physical functioning appear to be correlated more with increasing age than with classifiable nosological entities, and we entertain the possibility that, with increasing age, there are two forms of morbidity (the normal wear and tear of aging and diagnosed disease), which may vary independently. Next we examine the relationship between social and economic variables and the various self-reported measures of functioning. The measures of physical functioning and hospital use are not associated with any of the independent variables.

Some measures of family size and composition are associated with measures of psychosocial functioning among women over age 75, and symptoms of depression are associated with social isolation and the presence of impaired children in the camp.

Depression and hypertension are conditions often thought to be caused in part by a stressful social environment and are discussed in chapters 4 and 5. A simple scale measuring the prevalence of symptoms associated with depression was more sensitive to social variables than was clinical depression diagnosed from more extensive interviews. Hypertension was associated with measures of acculturation among women but not men.

The generally lower mortality rates of elderly Navajos, especially women, and the influence of social supports are discussed in chapter 6, which presents the mortality experience of the individuals in the sample over a three-year period. Although at present elderly Navajos may have a lesser burden of life-threatening illness than the non-Indian population, measures of dysfunction are similar, suggesting that the provision of long-term care and social services is an important issue facing the government and the tribe. The availability of these services for elderly Navajos and the question of who is responsible for providing them are discussed in chapter 7.

Finally, we examine the implications of the findings for health policy. To the extent that the situation in which the Navajos find themselves parallels that of the elderly nationwide, some of the difficulties facing the health system in the future are identified.

▸▸ 2 ◂◂

THE CHANGING CONTEXTS
OF AGING

THE PRESENT CHAPTER attempts to assess what is known about the
size and composition of cooperating kin groups prior to the destruction of the Navajo pastoral economy, which took place during the
1930s. Then, by following the fortunes of the descendents of one formerly large kin group, we examine the degree to which such groups
have deteriorated and how the social contexts of aging have changed
during the twenty-five-year period 1960–1984.

The Navajos' subsistence economy underwent several shifts during their history in the Southwest. By 1850, however, well over half
their subsistence was obtained from stock raising, and differences in
wealth had become marked (Aberle 1966:25). Pastoralism continued as
the major source of subsistence during the reservation period until the
stock reduction programs of the 1930s. After the reservation was established in 1868, 15,000 sheep and goats were distributed to approximately 7,500 Navajos. These holdings increased from approximately 2
head per capita in 1869 to over 65 during the 1880s and 1890s, when
sheep holdings were estimated at about one million and the population at 15,000 (Aberle 1966:30). Although stock holdings remained
high, the population continued to grow so that by 1930, just before the
stock reduction program began, there were approximately 39,000 Navajos and 1,370,000 sheep and goats. Per capita stock holdings had
dropped to 35.

Differences in wealth persisted during the entire period. In 1915 a survey of the southern Navajo reservation reported that 24 percent of families owned no sheep at all, and 42 percent had less than a hundred (*Navajo Yearbook* 1958:375). Aberle (1973:187) has reviewed the data for family composition and has concluded that, immediately prior to stock reduction, approximately 53 percent of all family units were independent nuclear families. There was, then as now, considerable regional variation: independent nuclear families constituted 22 percent of all camps at Navajo Mountain in 1938 and 48 percent at Klagetoh in 1936 (Collier 1951). These proportions are not much different from those reported for the western Navajo reservation during the 1970s, where single-family households accounted for 36 to 60 percent of total family units in all communities except the recently formed wage-work settlements near the Navajo Generating Station (Callaway et al. 1976:63).

From the foregoing it seems clear that even before the reservation period, the hardships of a seminomadic life and the unequal distribution of wealth served to make the positions of the elderly in all but the wealthy families somewhat insecure. Not only did the size and composition of cooperating kin groups vary but also, after the reservation was established, the quality of interpersonal relationships was not always supportive. Population density was low, and most Navajo families lived in isolation for much of the year. Economic survival was often precarious, and the early reservation years were marked by severe winters, droughts, and insect plagues that all too often led to hunger and near starvation. Kluckhohn (1962:93) concluded that tensions generated among members of the extended family were "hypertrophied by the emotional inbreeding" that the geographic isolation of Navaho households made almost inevitable. The presence of few opportunities to let off steam through socially approved behavior resulted in a "strong tendency toward involvement in a morbid nexus of emotional sensitivities from which there was little escape."

The multihousehold extended family appears not to have declined precipitously after the destruction of the pastoral economy, which suggests that it may not be a sensitive indicator of changes in the quality of life consequent upon the transition to wage work and that a more detailed examination of kin relations over time may be required.

THE COOPERATING KIN GROUP

The Kaibeto Plateau comprises the major portion of Land Management District 1 (LMD 1), the northern half of the Tuba City Service Unit sampled by this study. Henderson (1985) has reconstructed the history of the area, and his observations are used here as fairly representative of the entire service unit. The plateau was settled by two groups of Navajos immediately after their release from Fort Sumner and the establishment of the reservation in 1868. From that time until 1930 the population grew, augmented by migration from the eastern part of the reservation. Use of the range intensified, and the northern reaches of the plateau came to be favorite winter pasture, especially among the wealthy descendents of the original settlers. Differences in livestock holdings presumably increased throughout the period. By 1930 the area was more densely settled than in 1890. Families with larger flocks tended to travel greater distances between winter and summer locations, while families with smaller flocks had more restricted seasonal movements. The cooperating kin groups of the wealthy were larger than those of poorer stock owners. Most of the poorer families—perhaps as many as half of all the camps—cooperated little with kinsmen who were not resident in the camp.

The plateau relied more on livestock than other areas of the reservation, and there was a high degree of inequality in livestock holdings at the apogee of the livestock economy. In general, the "elite" was composed of families descended from the leaders of the Fort Sumner period, those of lower status were largely more recent immigrants, and those in the middle were from the poorer Ft. Sumner–period families as well as immigrant families. By the late 1930s the population of District 1 was between 1,300 and 1,700 individuals. Population density was about one person per square mile. There were between 164 and 221 camps, averaging about 7.6 members each. The elderly made up 4 percent of the population (Johnston 1966:157, 159); at most there were only 68 individuals age 65 or older. The majority of camps were nuclear families. The wealthiest owners, some 7 percent of all owners, held more than a third of all livestock in the district, the wealthiest 25 percent owned more than two thirds, and the poorest 50 percent, only 15 percent.

The differences in livestock holdings had a direct bearing on how people of the area lived. On the reservation generally, it was estimated that 250 sheep constituted a subsistence herd for a family of five; that is, 50 sheep per capita (Aberle 1966:84). In the 1930s, only District 1 showed average holdings (30–40 sheep) approaching subsistence needs. Nevertheless, only a quarter of the families maintained this necessary herd size. Perhaps an additional 25 percent of families with flocks of 250 to 500 head were at the margin of subsistence. The remaining 50 percent were poor or very poor. An even larger proportion of the families living in the other half of the area we studied (District 3) were poor. Wealthy families were, on average, larger because wealthy owners recruited members they already had the capacity to support.

An extensive strip of territory between Cow Springs in the south and Lechee to the north incorporated the seasonal migratory path of Crooked Finger, a grandson of one of the earliest settlers, and several of his consanguineal and affinal kin. Crooked Finger was the second wealthiest stock owner in the district, with a flock of between 2,500 and 3,000 head. By marrying a woman and her daughter from a less wealthy family, he gained access to some additional grazing land of good quality. During the summer he kept his flocks in the southern portion of his range, where he had fields near those of his maternal grandfather. During the winter he moved northwest of Kaibeto near Lechee. Several times in the early 1900s he wintered his flocks beyond the reservation boundary in southern Utah. Two of his sisters married a wealthy stockman, and Crooked Finger maintained close relations with them.

Crooked Finger never had any children of his own. His senior wife, however, had six children by her first marriage, all of whom served as herders. When these children reached maturity, he adopted some of their offspring and also reared some of his sister's children. Informants could recall more than twenty children reared by this prominent stock owner. Some of Crooked Finger's stepchildren and grandchildren married his sister's children, thus maintaining alliances between two very wealthy owners.

During the seasonal round, members of both families cooperated frequently in such activities as shearing and lambing. In addition, two of Crooked Finger's stepdaughters married a man named Falconer, who by the 1930s owned more than 1,000 head. Their camp was part of Crooked Finger's cooperating unit on a year-round basis. On some occasions then, the combined flocks of Crooked Finger and his sisters were well in excess of 4,500 head. Crooked Finger's position was further enhanced by the fact that he was a ceremonialist. His two step-daughters became hand-trembler diagnosticians, and their husband, Falconer, was also a ceremonialist.

The wealthy owned enough livestock to pay for expensive cere-monial treatments when they were ill and controlled better and more extensive rangeland, so they were more insulated from the vagaries of the weather. Crooked Finger's brother-in-law, for example, once spon-sored a nine-night Nightway ceremony that included thirty dance teams. Each team received one sheep. About another hundred sheep were slaughtered to feed the numerous guests, many of whom came from beyond the local community. Sponsoring large ceremonies was a means of transforming surplus stock wealth into prestige. In addi-tion, many wealthy owners hired poor men to help as herders. Poorer families, already at the margin of subsistence, could not recover as quickly from the depletion of their stock holdings caused by bad weather or the expense of ceremonial cures.

After livestock reduction, there were no longer any wealthy fami-lies, only the poor and the very poor. There was no longer any reason for wealthy families to undertake long seasonal moves. These shifts in residence had been one of the prime means by which families kept in contact over long distances. Families that summered together and cooperated in farming no longer had any economic reason to move to winter pasture, where they would cooperate with a different config-uration of kin. With smaller flocks there was less need for manpower. Sheep shearing and lambing operations were no longer occasions that required the cooperation of more than a few families. The nature of relations between the wealthy and those of lesser means was altered; there were no longer any wealthy owners to whom the poor could turn for temporary herding and construction work. The wealthy had not only lost their ability to sell their surplus in the market, they also had no surplus to redistribute locally through generosity or the spon-sorship of ceremonials.

After stock reduction, Crooked Finger and his children remained near their farms in the southern portion of the district. Even the winter graze they still needed to use was eventually denied them as the population grew and more grazing district lines were drawn. In-creasingly, grazing land was in short supply even for the small flocks of a few hundred head that some of the families were still able to maintain. Crooked Finger's "outfit" no longer cooperated with his sisters'. Herds, in fact, had become so small that there was no longer a compelling need for several camps to cooperate regularly.

By 1960, when we first became acquainted with Crooked Finger, the extended families that comprised the outfit had already drifted apart. Crooked Finger's sisters' children remained north of Kaibeto, and Falconer's senior wife and several of her adult children had disassociated themselves only the year before, following a dispute about attending peyote ceremonies. Nevertheless, four camps constituted a "core" of regularly interacting families, and four other camps cooperated with this core on a less regular basis. Together the eight camps included 21 households, with a total population of 105, of which 64 were minor children. Crooked Finger, Falconer, Falconer's son, Rex, and an adopted granddaughter, Bridget, headed the four most closely cooperating camps. The remaining four camps were headed by one of Crooked Finger's stepsons, who was also Bridget's father, and three of his adult children, one of whom had also been adopted by Crooked Finger.

Crooked Finger, his two wives, and an adopted deaf-mute granddaughter with her ceremonialist husband and children lived together in one camp. By this time Crooked Finger was about 92 years old; his first wife was over 80, and his second wife was in her mid 60s. Falconer was about 70 years old in 1960, and his wife was four years younger. Their two daughters with their husbands and children constituted the other households of the camp. Their son, Rex, lived about a quarter of a mile away with his younger brother, each with their wives and children. Bridget, who lived about a mile away with her crippled husband, four minor children, and three married daughters and their families, was the link between the Crooked Finger and Falconer camps and those of her father, Begashie, then 72 years of age, her brother, and two half sisters. Each of these camps contained the households of the senior couples and one or two of their married daughters.

In the early 1960s the eight camps owned a total of 1,890 sheep.[1] This was an average of 18 head per capita, well below the amount necessary to support a family. Unearned income from social security and Aid to Families with Dependent Children was a major source of income. None of the younger men had steady work, although several worked for a few months each year away from the reservation. The average annual per capita income from all sources was about $360.

Few economic activities demanded the cooperation of all or most of the camps. Shearing was most often done within a single camp or by two cooperating camps. Similarly, there was no need to pool the flocks of several camps during the lambing season. Gelding horses was the only ranching activity we were able to document that involved men from all the camps. There were still seasonal moves to winter pasture, but these involved single households leaving the camps to take the flocks a few miles to the north. Transportation was a major problem, however. Only Rex owned a truck, and this was used extensively by the four core camps for hauling wood and water and for trips to town, trading post, and hospital. The other four camps relied on help from neighbors and from children who lived off-reservation but who came home weekends to help out. Most of the camps worked small dry farms that did not require assistance from outside the extended family. Crooked Finger's fields in Cow Springs Canyon, however, were more extensive and better watered. During planting, five families from four camps stayed with Crooked Finger in the canyon until the job was done. A similar pattern was followed during the harvest, which was shared among all the camps that had contributed labor.

Most of the curing ceremonies involved only a single camp, or one camp with the assistance of individuals from another. Because there were three ceremonialists in the kin group, many of the sings were "in-house" affairs, with only a few relatives coming to attend rather than to help out. The only ceremonies that called for hosting large numbers of guests were three Enemy Way sings given by three different camps during the early years of the decade. Each of these events involved six of the eight camps as well as clan relatives of the patient. Between 1956 and 1960, 80 ceremonies were performed for adults of the eight camps. For the period 1965–1969, the total number of ceremonies remained the same, but 62 (77 percent) were peyote meetings. For all but two of the adults this did not represent a religious conversion so much as a shift to a cheaper and shorter (one-night) healing ceremony that required little cooperation from kinsmen (Levy and Kunitz 1974:129).

By the early 1970s, the kin group, which had 21 households in 1960, had shrunk to 11 households grouped into 6 camps. The Crooked Finger and Falconer camps had both disintegrated. Crooked Finger and his wives had died. The deaf-mute granddaughter, deserted by her husband, left to live with a married sister. Falconer's youngest daughter and her family left the reservation for wage work. The older daughter and her husband had been killed in an automobile accident.

Their children went to live with Rex, as did Falconer's wife after his death. A total of 9 adults had died by 1973, and several newly formed families had left the area to obtain wage work. Four families had moved some distance away but were still able to visit often and to help when needed. The decrease in the number of households was due as much to the emigration of younger couples as it was to death.

Among the 47 adults 21 years of age and older in 1967, only 6 had steady wage work, and 7 combined seasonal wage work with stock-raising (Levy and Kunitz 1974:115). Twenty-nine (57 percent) thought of themselves as full-time stockraisers. Only 5 (10 percent) were re-tired or unemployed and receiving social welfare or social security payments. By 1973 the number of retired and unemployed had risen to 33 percent, and although the proportion of adults with wage work had not changed, as many women as men had steady employment. Most striking was the growth in the number of women heads of household—from 1 in 1960 to 4 in 1973. The younger adults who remained at home were most often divorced mothers with their de-pendent children. Of the 6 camps, only Rex's had households headed by active males with wage work. This was also the largest camp, containing 3 households. Three camps were comprised of 2 house-holds each; 3 of these 6 households were headed by unemployed women, and 3 were headed by unemployed men, 1 of whom had an employed single daughter. The two single-household camps were headed by a widow and a retired stockraiser, Begashie, who then lived alone with his wife.

The decline in the number of sheep per capita (from 18 to 16) was not appreciable. Nor did the economic profile of the six camps differ radically from that of the surrounding area. The average annual per capita income for the group ($749) was only $100 less, although pur-chasing power had declined appreciably due to inflation. The propor-tion of the total derived from wage work (40 percent) and unearned income (50 percent) was the inverse of the community average (Calla-way et al. 1976:67). Wealth differences among the camps had become marked, however. Rex's camp derived 76 percent of its total income from all sources from wage work and had a per capita income of $1,098. In sharp contrast, the camp of the widow and her divorced daughter relied primarily on unearned income and had a per capita income of $491. It is abundantly clear that social security and welfare had become the major means of support for several families.

THE DECLINE OF THE ELDERLY

Although no longer wealthy, the older members of the kin group lived in camps that included several of their married children. In February 1960, Crooked Finger and his wives decided to transfer their sheep permits to some of their children and grandchildren and to join Falconer's camp. This event marked Crooked Finger's transition from leader to dependent aged, and coincidentally it was during this year that the health status of the trio also began to decline.

Crooked Finger and his wives had been active and healthy up to this time. Crooked Finger frequently herded sheep on horseback and had occasion to visit the hospital for the first time only in 1958, when he sought treatment for a sore on his head. A note was made at this time that he had generalized arthritis. The older wife was seen at the hospital for the first time in 1959. Her daughter, Crooked Finger's second wife, had been seen as early as 1949 for chronic otitis media and for arthritis in an elbow. Between 1955 and 1958 she had been seen several times for diarrhea, otitis media, meningitis, arteriosclerosis, and osteoarthritis of the lower spine, and in 1959 she was diagnosed as suffering from adult-onset diabetes. Of the three, then, only the youngest had any serious health problems requiring the attention of the family.

During the winter of 1960, Crooked Finger complained of dysuria and was seen in hospital, where he was found to have cystitis and prostatitis. He remained quite active, however, herding sheep and chopping wood although his arthritic fingers were quite gnarled and difficult to use. By the end of the winter he complained frequently about his health, as did his first wife, who was also quite active. While conducting a ceremony he began to feel weak and began to think of giving up his activities as a ceremonialist.

The younger wife was sent away for evaluation of her eyesight in May, but the recommended cataract operation had to be postponed until her diabetes could be brought under control. Her condition presented problems because someone in the family had to administer injections of insulin and bring her to hospital frequently to be monitored. By early spring they were living by their farms in the canyon, which made these frequent trips difficult. Both wives underwent cataract operations during the summer and seemed to be doing well in the canyon camp, but in September Crooked Finger became ill suddenly with a kidney infection and prostate problems and was brought to hospital in a wagon. The family was told he was too old for prostate surgery, and they decided that his wives and he should give up sheep herding and move in with Bridget so that it would be easier to get them to hospital when the need arose. Later in the month, Crooked Finger also decided he would no longer conduct ceremonies and gave his ceremonial paraphernalia to a clan "nephew."

The ability of several cooperating camps to assume responsibility for the care of the elderly made it possible for economic pursuits to continue uninterrupted. In October, after Crooked Finger fainted while on horseback, the family decided that his wives, the deaf-mute granddaughter, and he should return to the Falconer camp, which was no longer in the canyon, because they had access to Rex's truck and could get him to hospital faster than Bridget could. At the end of the year, Crooked Finger was found to have active tuberculosis after he was circumcised in an effort to alleviate problems with urinary retention. At that time he was sent home on Isoniazid therapy. The sanitorium at Fort Defiance was no longer in use, so he would either have to be cared for at home or sent off the reservation to Tucson. The physicians, fearing he was too old and weak to survive such a journey, wanted him to be kept at home in "semi-isolation." Unfortunately, the Falconer temporary winter camp consisted of only one hogan, a tent, and a brush arbor. On cold nights as many as twenty people would be crowded into the single hogan. A compromise was reached while the family discussed the matter, and Crooked Finger was kept in hospital until the snow cleared. By January 1961, Bridget had agreed to take the old people again because, although she also had to care for her crippled husband, she did have more room. During the rest of the winter, Crooked Finger and his wives were preoccupied with their health problems. For the first time, "the old folks were scared, scared to get old and scared to die."

With the return of warm weather, Crooked Finger, his wives, and their deaf-mute granddaughter returned to Falconer's camp. Then in June they joined one of Bridget's married daughters by the fields in Cow Springs Canyon, and it was there that the first wife, now in her late eighties, died unexpectedly. Everyone had gone to the trading post that day except for the old people. She had been busy all morning washing dishes and doing other chores. In the afternoon she sat under a tree in front of the hogan, preparing some herbs. Crooked Finger passed her on his way to the corral on his horse and heard her say, "I am going now." He went toward her and asked what she meant, but she wouldn't answer. He then went and got the sheep from the corral and took them out. Later, on the way back, he saw she was lying down on a blanket. He put all the sheep back into the corral and then, when he returned, found that she was dead. Crooked Finger had no one to help him, so he rode over to Bridget's camp and got the older children to help. The police were called, and she was buried in the canyon. Everyone then moved up to Bridget's camp to stay. Although Bridget's daughter and the deaf-mute woman returned to the fields later that summer, the old people were kept with Bridget so that they could be taken to the hospital as the need arose.

Crooked Finger continued to have fainting episodes until, in 1962, a prostate operation was performed. Subsequently, he was frequently disoriented and required bed rails to keep him from leaving hospital. One night this precaution was overlooked, and he broke his hip trying to get out of bed. The hip was repaired, but he never regained his senses and died in hospital soon after at 94 years of age.

The younger wife declined slowly for another year. Diabetes caused abscesses on her leg, and gangrene set in. The foot was in danger of amputation, but the end came before this was necessary. She died in the winter of 1963–64 at age 69.

Falconer, who visited the hospital for the first time in 1961, continued in good health until the winter of 1967–68, when he contracted pneumonia. Ceremonial treatments and several visits to the clinic at Page, Arizona, were made until, early in 1968, he was brought to hospital in Tuba City, where he died at age 76.

During the years Bridget was caring for her grandparents, she was also providing for her crippled husband, Simon, who had sustained a spinal cord injury after a riding accident in 1956 when he was 62 years old. The injury caused a partial quadriplegia and was soon followed by chronic cystitis and severe arthritis of the hands, at one time diagnosed as rheumatoid. By 1960 the hospital chart noted malnutrition, extreme wasting, and senility due to lack of care. Increasing his mobility would have required a long stay in an off-reservation facility and the will to continue a regimen of exercise and physical therapy after his return. Simon was never willing to leave home for any length of time and seemed uninterested in maintaining an exercise regimen. In our opinion, it is doubtful that his wife had the time to devote to this task in any event. Simon was maintained at home for eighteen years, declining gradually until, no longer able to eat, he was taken to hospital, where he died in 1973 when he was 79 years old.

Begashie, Bridget's father, was 95 years old when he died in 1983. For several years he and his wife, who was 25 years his junior, had been living alone. Their widowed daughter had moved away permanently during the 1960s to avoid having their winter grazing area occupied by newcomers. His son, who had lived off-reservation for many years, had returned and was living some miles away near the school where he had a job. He was able to return to his parents' camp on most weekends to help with the heavier chores and to provide transportation when necessary, and his wife came by once a week to bring water and to see if they needed a ride to the clinic or trading post. Nevertheless, the elderly couple had no way to get to hospital in the event of an emergency. Begashie was in good health, although he had undergone a gall bladder operation at age 93 and had lost most of his eyesight. The couple cared for their son's sheep and received old-age benefits. The end came at home without any warning. There was never any evidence of depression or withdrawal from social contact, and it is doubtful that the living arrangements contributed measurably to his decline. After Begashie's death, his widow went to live with her son, and the campsite was abandoned.

Hashkie, Falconer's next to youngest son, was 50 years old in 1960 and was married to one of Bridget's daughters. He was the only male of the group to spend his final years living alone while caring for his minor children. For several years after his marriage, Hashkie stayed away from his wife, claiming that he was divorced. He did return and live with her in Bridget's camp for more than ten years, during which time they had several children. The marriage was not very happy, due in part to the fact that Hashkie was almost thirty years older than his wife, who later left him. For about five or six years after this, Hashkie lived alone with three of the children in a hogan near the road not more than a quarter mile from Rex's camp. In 1982, two of the children were in boarding school. Hashkie had part-time work at the school attended by the youngest child, with whom he caught the school bus on the days he worked. He owned ten sheep and one cow, which were cared for by Rex, and he received $4,000 per year from his job and from social security. After a year of heart problems, he underwent triple bypass surgery but died soon after at age 73.

Between 1961 and 1985, then, seven elderly people in the extended kin group died. All died of natural causes and all but one were above the age of 73. This contrasts sharply with the four men and one woman below the age of 65 who died during the same period, all from accidents. Two of the older people, Simon and Crooked Finger's younger wife, required a considerable amount of attention. The question arises whether the conditions of life on the reservation precluded a standard of care modern physicians would consider adequate. We were impressed by the amount of control over their daily activities these old people were able to maintain and by the supportiveness of those who cared for them. As long as their physical condition permitted, Crooked Finger, his wives, and Falconer continued to perform any tasks they felt capable of, including herding and chopping wood. The youngest children assisted Simon and Crooked Finger's younger wife to leave the hogan to relieve themselves, and they were left alone as little as possible.

On the other hand, there were occasions when they were unattended for varying periods of time. There was no running water and only a fire for heat. With some families away herding, a trip to the trading post or for firewood not infrequently necessitated that the infirm be left behind. There were occasions when neither of them could keep the fire going, so they spent hours in the cold. There were also many days when the insulin injections were forgotten. Communication and transportation were persistent problems. There were no phones to use to call for help and, with only one truck shared among four camps, it was usually not possible to get to hospital quickly. Nor was it possible to provide a wide range of foods the older people could eat. The diet was the typical one of fried bread, mutton, potatoes, and coffee. Fresh fruit and vegetables were not often consumed, although corn and melons were available in season. It was easy to become undernourished after chewing became a chore. Add to these constraints the Navajos' fear of being sent away from home to hospitals where no one spoke their language and it is easy to see how long-term care at home might not meet with the approval of many health care providers. Moreover, the families we were acquainted with were atypical with respect to the number of extended families in the network. Those who had always been less affluent could mobilize far fewer resources; for them caring for the elderly presented even more formidable problems than those we have recounted.

Even in this formerly wealthy set of related families the disintegration of the kin group was, we have seen, well advanced by the early 1980s. Two of the older people who died during the 1970s and 1980s lived in relative isolation, although this probably had little to do with their decline. In 1985 there were ten households grouped into seven camps, only two of which contained more than one household. Five households were headed by men, three of whom were over 65 years of age. Three of the five households headed by women were led by active widows, two of whom had divorced daughters and minor children living with them. Four of the camps were totally dependent on welfare and social security. Bridget, for example, after years of caring for others, was 77 years old and living with a divorced daughter and granddaughter and their young children. Altogether there were ten in the camp subsisting on approximately $580 per capita from Aid to Families with Dependent Children, social security, and a herd of only forty-eight sheep and six cattle.

Routine cooperation with relatives in other camps is a thing of the past. Anglo-style family reunions celebrating an older person's birthday and Thanksgiving dinners are the only occasions attended by relatives from other camps. These expressions of sentiment, however, are not satisfactory substitutes for the sense of kin solidarity that once provided the elderly with support and security. Among the older people there is, according to one of Bridget's daughters, a pervasive sense of sadness and loss as well as a nostalgia for the time when Navajos were self-sufficient and in control of their lives. The older people feel that they are doing no more than surviving together, and even the mother-daughter bond is gradually weakening.

In sum, social support provided by kinsmen was predicated on the possession of sizeable stock holdings prior to stock reduction. Camp size was only one measure of this support, the other being regular cooperation among a number of related camps. We speak here only of the wealthy, for even before stock reduction approximately 50 percent of all families in the Tuba City Service Unit lived in single-household camps. Presumably they were less able to rely on kin for support even then than were those who controlled a great deal of wealth.

The stock reduction programs destroyed the pastoral economy without providing an alternative means of making a living. It was not until the 1960s that most children in an age cohort were receiving an education preparing them for wage work. But wage work opportunities existed almost exclusively in off-reservation towns or agency towns on the reservation. In consequence, the better educated, newly formed families most often had to leave their homes to make a living. Today, intercamp cooperation is virtually nonexistent, and multi-household camps are all too frequently composed of families headed by the unemployed and those employed only part-time. The elderly may live out their declining years in impoverished camps with limited capabilities, or alternately may be required to move in with employed children living at some distance from the home community. The subsistence economy is still, 50 years after stock reduction, as much dependent on unearned as on earned income.

With this historical perspective in mind, we may now turn to a more detailed examination of the health status of the elderly people in our sample in the 1980s. There is every indication that health conditions and the health delivery system are in a state of flux and that the next quarter of a century will witness a number of important changes.

▸▸ 3 ◂◂

SOCIAL ORGANIZATION, MORBIDITY, AND HOSPITAL USE

IN THIS CHAPTER we deal with two related issues. The first is the association between morbidity and hospital utilization. This is a particularly important topic because, as we discuss in more detail in chapter 6, the Navajos are one of those populations in which a mortality "crossover" is observed. That is, compared with Anglo-Americans, Navajos' mortality rates are higher at young ages and lower in old age. It has been speculated that, in such populations, people who survive into old age are healthier than people of the same age in populations with low mortality among the young, the reason being that among people like the Navajo the frail would die early, leaving behind a hardy residual group (Markides and Machalek 1984).

The second issue is the impact of social organization on both morbidity and hospital utilization, which is the central concern of this study. The literature on social supports and health suggests that the availability of family and friends results in good health and low use of formal health care institutions. There is some reason to think, however, that families may create stressful situations that could conceivably result in a diminution in health status and/or increased dependence on formal organizations. The fact that the multihousehold extended family, or camp, persists on the Navajo reservation despite an increased reliance on wage work and a decline in the traditional pastoral economy suggests that it is still the key to survival for many Navajos.

Economic conditions may constrain individuals' choices, forcing them to live with relatives even if the arrangement is stressful.

THE SELF-REPORTED LEVEL OF FUNCTIONING AND THE USE OF HEALTH CARE

The number of elderly Navajos hospitalized each year has increased slowly since 1972, whereas the average length of a hospital stay has decreased very dramatically (Kunitz 1983). Hospital discharges increased about 21 percent—from 1,431 in FY 1972 to 1,735 in CY 1982—while the average length of a stay declined about 44 percent from 15.1 to 8.4 days. The impact on total patient days was substantial, amounting to a decline of about 33 percent, from 21,608 days to 14,523. The average annual discharge rate between 1980 and 1984 was somewhere between 219 and 267 per 1,000, considerably lower than the rate for the general U.S. population, which increased from 355 to 399 per 1,000 from 1977 to 1982 (Waldo and Lazenby 1984:7).

Navajos have higher discharge rates for infective and parasitic diseases than do the elderly in the general population (Table 3.1). For all other categories, the Navajo rates are either lower or the same. Of the three most important categories for Navajos—diseases of the circulatory, respiratory, and digestive systems—the latter two occur at about the same rate as in the general population, and the first occurs at a substantially lower rate. These diagnostic patterns are approximately what one would expect, based on the distribution of causes of death (see chapter 6). Circulatory diseases and neoplasms are less significant among Navajos than they are among the general population. Diseases of the respiratory system cover a wide assortment of infectious and noninfectious maladies. Among Navajos, influenza and pneumonia are especially important as causes of both mortality and hospitalized morbidity. With the available data it is difficult to be certain how the non-Navajo discharge pattern of respiratory diseases may differ.

Infectious diseases, while still significant among the elderly Navajos, are no longer the leading cause of mortality and hospitalized morbidity. Although respiratory diseases (primarily influenza and pneumonias) are the single leading discharge diagnosis, circulatory diseases consume more hospital days. Indeed, average lengths of stay differ significantly among primary diagnostic categories ($p < 0.001$ by

Table 3.1. Hospital Discharge Diagnoses, Average Length of Stay, and Average Annual Discharge Rates of Navajos Age 65 and Above, FY 1980–1983

First Listed Discharge Diagnoses	No. of Discharges	ALOS	Total No. of Days	Average Annual rate/1,000		U.S. rate/1,000 1982 (Age 65 and above)[c]
				Low[a]	High[b]	
Infective and parasitic	334	9.7	3,227	11.4	13.9	5
Neoplasms	423	10.9	4,600	14.5	17.6	42
Endocrine, etc.	270	8.8	2,385	9.2	11.3	16
Diseases of blood, etc.	56	9.9	552	1.9	2.3	6
Mental disorders	101	9.8	987	3.5	4.2	10
Diseases of the nervous system	478	6.4	3,043	16.4	19.9	28
Circulatory system	863	8.9	7,734	29.5	35.9	117
Respiratory system	1,005	6.9	6,948	34.4	41.9	37
Digestive system	827	7.8	6,474	28.3	34.4	50
Genitourinary system	579	7.7	4,460	19.8	24.1	28
Skin and subcutaneous tissue	161	13.2	2,124	5.5	6.7	5
Musculo-skeletal	118	10.3	1,211	4.0	4.9	22
Congenital anomalies	10	6.2	62	0.3	0.4	1.0
Symptoms, etc.	434	6.2	2,711	14.9	18.1	3.0
Accidents, etc.	522	9.2	4,801	17.9	21.8	28.0
Special conditions, tests, etc.	222	9.9	2,195	7.6	9.3	2.0

[a]Low rate based upon population estimate of 7,300.
[b]High rate based upon population estimate of 6,000.
Source: Waldo and Lazenby 1984:9.

analysis of variance), and of the three most significant rubrics, respiratory diseases require significantly shorter lengths of stay than the others (using Duncan's multiple range test). This is surprising, considering that the average age of patients with respiratory diseases is significantly greater than that of patients with either digestive (mostly gall bladder) or circulatory diseases—78.7 for the former versus 76.7 for the latter two. In fact, neither age nor sex is related to length of stay ($p > 0.57$ by analysis of covariance).

The fact that elderly Navajos have lower rates of hospitalization and mortality supports the notion that their health may indeed be better than that of non-Indians of the same age. Because morbidity may have a number of components, however, it is also possible that the survivors in poor populations in which a mortality crossover is observed may experience the same decreasing levels of function as their age mates in more affluent populations but without suffering from a variety of life-threatening ills. For example, Markides and Machalek (1984) found that American Indians in general manifest the same mortality crossover phenomenon as the Navajos and that the elderly tend to have lower rates of hospitalization than people of the same age in the general population. Yet survey data from a nationwide sample of elderly Indians indicate less ability to perform activities of daily living (ambulation and dressing and feeding oneself, for example) than is observed among non-Indians (NICOA 1981a:130–134). The issue is important because it is sometimes thought that the increased survival of older people in the larger society means that an expanding proportion of the elderly will be unfit and will require an increasingly disproportionate share of the resources of the service sector. It may also be interpreted to mean that elderly American Indians do not need the same kind of supportive services as elderly Anglo-Americans.

In this section we consider measures of health status: medical diagnoses gleaned from informants' medical records; the self-reported level of functioning based on standardized scales, the Sickness Impact Profile (SIP); hospital use immediately prior to and during the study period (January 1, 1980–June 30, 1983); and the interrelations among them.

The SIP scales are of two sorts: (1) physical mobility and self-care, and (2) psychosocial functioning.[1] High scores reflect many affirmative answers and indicate worse levels of functioning. Three scales measure the domain of physical mobility and self-care: Ambulation

(AMBSIP), Mobility (MOBSIP), and Body Care and Movement (BCMSIP). Two scales comprise the domain of psychosocial functioning: Alertness Behavior (ALBSIP) and Social Interaction (SOISIP). The three scales measuring physical mobility are summed to provide a total score of physical functioning (PHYSIP). All five scales summed provide a measure of the Total Sickness Impact Profile (TOTSIP). The purpose of these scales is to assess the levels of function as they relate to health status, not to make a diagnosis of a medically classifiable disease.

Means were always higher than medians, and the very large differences for some of the scales indicate the presence of extreme values that may make the use of parametric statistical tests questionable.[2] In some of the analyses, therefore, we have done nonparametric analyses instead of, or in addition to, parametric. Thus we use ordinal rather than interval variables. Women below 75 years of age always reported better levels of function than those 75 and above. Men's scores in each group tended to be more nearly the same, sometimes resembling the younger women and at other times the older. Within each age-sex group, all the scales were highly correlated.[3]

The measures of hospital utilization for the study period included number of hospitalizations, total number of days in hospital, average length of hospital stay, number of surgical procedures, and number of laboratory tests performed.[4] Ninety-four people in the sample were hospitalized a total of 175 times between January 1, 1980, and June 30, 1983. Women below the age of 75 were hospitalized significantly less often (18/22: χ^2 = 9.29; df = 3; p = .025) than the older women (27/62) and any of the men (27/70 and 22/54, respectively), which is not surprising, given their lower SIP scores.

Although the measures of hospital use are continuous variables, most of the people in the sample were not hospitalized during the study period, and it would therefore be inappropriate to consider them all together when correlating the SIP scales with the measures of hospital use. Instead, we have first compared the people who were hospitalized with those who were not and then examined the hospitalized group's patterns of utilization.

A logistic regression with age, sex, and PHYSIP as the independent variables and whether hospitalized or not as the dependent variable shows that only the level of physical functioning (PHYSIP score) is significantly associated with hospital use (Table 3.2). When, however, ALBSIP and then SOISIP are substituted for PHYSIP, age is signifi-

Table 3.2. Logistic Regression of Hospital Use During 1980–1983 Adjusted for Age, Sex, and PHYSIP

Age	Male		Female	
	Low PHYSIP[a]	High PHYSIP[a]	Low PHYSIP[a]	High PHYSIP[a]
Below age 75	9/36	16/32	6/52	12/30
Age 75 and above	7/24	15/30	6/20	21/40

Parameter	Estimate	S.E.	Odds Scale	95% Confidence Interval
Age	0.43	0.27	1.53	(0.90, 2.64)
Sex	−0.31	0.27	0.73	(0.43, 1.26)
PHYSIP	1.81	0.27	6.11	(3.56, 10.49)

[a]The numerator is the number in a particular age-sex group who were hospitalized. The denominator is the number in that age-sex-PHYSIP group.

cantly associated with hospitalization, because most people with high PHYSIP scores are older than those with low scores.

When only those who were hospitalized are considered, we find that the measures of hospital use are significantly correlated within each age-sex group but that significant relationships between these measures and the SIP scores are found only among men and women less than 75 years of age (Table 3.3). How are these differences between age groups to be explained?

Despite the fact that people 75 and older tended to have higher PHYSIP scores, it was the younger patients who were most often hospitalized for 40 or more days during the study period, whether or not they had high PHYSIP scores.[5] People with extremely high PHYSIP scores (the top 10 percent) and low hospital use were almost invariably 75 years of age or above (Table 3.4). These patterns are largely explained by the fact that the SIP scales measure self-reported level of functioning, not specific diseases.

Among the eight people hospitalized for 40 days or more were four women below the age of 75. One had suffered a severe stroke, which left her disabled. She had spent much time in hospital and was interviewed at home shortly before being placed in a nursing home. Another had a long history of alcohol abuse and had recently de-

Table 3.3. Pearson's *r* Correlations of Hospital and SIP Variables (Hospitalized Respondents Only)

	Days in Hosp.	Number of Tests	Number of Hosp.	PHYSIP	ALBSIP	SOISIP
A. Men[a]						
Days in hospital	—	.94	.87	.13	-.11	-.13
Number of tests	.89	—	.78	.10	-.10	-.10
Number of hospitalizations	.48	.35	—	.07	-.21	-.21
PHYSIP	.47	.31	.71	—	.43	.31
ALBSIP	.10	.05	.46	.35	—	.45
SOISIP	.26	.21	.29	.26	.74	—

Men below age 75: $r = .46$ $p = .01$

Men age 75 and above: $r = .51$ $p = .01$

	Days in Hosp.	Number of Tests	Number of Hosp.	PHYSIP	ALBSIP	SOISIP
B. Women[b]						
Days in hospital	—	.83	.44	-.03	-.08	-.14
Number of tests	.45	—	.49	-.21	-.13	-.22
Number of hospitalizations	.36	.85	—	.01	.12	.09
PHYSIP	.25	.77	.59	—	.70	.80
ALBSIP	.28	.65	.60	.78	—	.80
SOISIP	.25	.75	.53	.92	.71	—

Women below age 75: $r = .45$ $p = .05$

Women age 75 and above: $r = .44$ $p = .02$

[a]Men below age 75 are below the diagonal ($N = 43$). Men age 75 and above are above the diagonal ($N = 32$).
[b]Women below age 75 are below the diagonal ($N = 64$). Women age 75 and above are above the diagonal ($N = 35$).

veloped active tuberculosis. She was not disabled but had spent four months in hospital. A third had lost several close relatives during the preceding several years and had subsequently gone into a severe depression, which was compounded by Parkinson's disease and an organic brain syndrome. She was living with relatives and appeared stable when interviewed. The fourth woman had once had tuberculosis, which left her with little functioning lung. She was in and out of hospital with episodes of respiratory failure.

Table 3.4. Hospital Use and PHYSIP Scores by Age

	Age	
	Below 75	*75 and Above*
A. PHYSIP low, hospital low	32	36
B. PHYSIP high,[a] hospital low	1	12
C. PHYSIP low, hospital high[b]	5	0
D. PHYSIP high, hospital high	2	1

A × B, χ^2 = 5.4, $p < .02$
B × C, $p < .005$ (Fisher's exact test)
B × D, not significant
(A + B) × (C + D), χ^2 = 4.68, $p < .05$
Unknowns omitted

[a]High PHYSIP = top 10 percent
[b]High hospital = 40 days over study period

One of the three men below the age of 75 who had spent much time in hospital also had old tuberculosis and numerous episodes of respiratory failure. Like the woman described above, he required oxygen at home and was severely disabled. He also suffered from diabetes and hypertension. The second man suffered from diabetes and chronic renal failure, for which he required frequent dialysis. He had also lost both legs in an accident many years before and was confined to a wheelchair. The third had a long history of tuberculosis in addition to benign essential hypertension and diabetes. His lengthy hospitalization, however, was due to the development of peritonitis, which required rather extensive abdominal surgery. The only person above the age of 75 with 40 or more days in hospital was a man of 83 who had tuberculosis (old), diabetes, congestive heart failure, eczema, cellulitis, and urinary tract infections.

By way of contrast, consider the thirteen people with extremely high PHYSIP scores and less than 40 days of hospital use. One woman younger than 75 was seriously disabled from an old hip fracture. She also had diabetes and mild congestive heart failure and had suffered a pulmonary embolism. She had been hospitalized a total of 19 days. The other twelve were all 75 or older. Three had chronic brain syndrome, six had severe osteoarthritis, one had a combination of chronic brain syndrome and osteoarthritis, and two had Parkinson's disease.

To simplify the characterization of the people with low PHYSIP scores and low hospital use, we shall discuss only those with more than 10 but less than 40 days of hospitalization (9 men and 4 women below age 75; 7 men and 10 women 75 or older). Among the nine men below age 75 were two admitted with benign prostatic hypertrophy. Four were admitted with pneumonia, one of whom still suffered symptoms from an earlier subdural hematoma, another had chronic nephritis and rheumatoid arthritis, a third had congestive heart failure, emphysema, and bronchiectasis, and the last had diabetes and hypertension. The seventh had an acute myocardial infarction; the eighth had gout, rheumatoid arthritis, and ankylosis of several joints; and the ninth had old tuberculous osteomyelitis requiring surgery and chemotherapy. Among the four women in this age group was one who had had epilepsy since childhood and who experienced recurrent generalized seizures that on one occasion caused her to fall into a fire and receive serious burns. Another had gall bladder disease; a third had been admitted for diarrhea, osteoarthritis, and panhypopituitarism resulting from an earlier postpartum hemorrhage. The fourth had diabetes, uterine prolapse, and a urinary tract infection.

Among the seven older men were three admitted for pneumonia. One also had gall bladder disease, another had old tuberculosis, and the third had diabetes. Another man had renal calculi and benign prostatic hypertrophy. The fifth had burns of the face and hand, the sixth a fractured femur, and the seventh, with more than 30 days in hospital, was diagnosed simply as senile. Two of the older women had pneumonia, in addition to which one had gall bladder disease and the other emphysema. A third had gall bladder disease and bubonic plague. Two women had ischemic heart disease, two others had cholecystitis, another had diarrhea, and the last had hypertension, poorly defined cerebrovascular disease, diabetes, and diverticulitis.

This lengthy litany should help make clear why the correlations between SIP and hospital utilization are significant for the men and women below the age of 75 but not for those who were older. Among the younger group were a few extreme cases, people who suffered from severe chronic diseases that required much time in hospital and also caused very substantial functional impairment. It is these extreme cases that made the correlations significant. Among those 75 and older were many people with considerable loss of function not caused by conditions that, in the Navajo setting, result in extremes of hospital use.

We may be observing a cohort effect. The younger group includes a few people with diseases of sufficient severity that in all likelihood they will not survive beyond their late seventies. The older cohort, on the other hand, seems to have already lost such individuals, and those who have survived are impaired in a variety of ways that make them dependent on help different from that provided in a general hospital.

It is, of course, possible that among the people who were not hospitalized there were people as sick as those we found needing substantial levels of hospital care. In fact, however, people with extreme PHYSIP scores in the 90th percentile who were not hospitalized were no different from those with equally high scores who were hospitalized less than 40 days. Eleven people were in this category, four below the age of 75 and seven 75 and above. Three of the younger respondents had osteoarthritis, two of whom also had diabetes, while the third had a crippled limb caused by what was presumed to have been childhood paralytic polio. The fourth had Parkinson's disease. Among those 75 and above were four people with severe osteoarthritis, two of whom were also senile. A fifth and sixth were each blind, deaf, and occasionally confused. The seventh had very severe rheumatoid arthritis.

As noted previously, it has been speculated that populations in which a mortality crossover is observed experience some sort of selection process such that people who survive into old age are more fit than people of the same age in populations in which mortality at young ages is low. This would be especially convincing if populations in which the crossover is observed died young of the same problems that account for the mortality at old age. This is, in fact, not the case. Death among the young tends to be from such "exogenous" factors as infectious diseases and accidents, whereas among the elderly death is primarily due to "endogenous" causes such as cardiovascular disease (Nam et al. 1978; Weatherby et al. 1983; Wing et al. 1985). On the other hand, one might argue that the risk-taking behavior that leads some young people to die of violent causes may be related to the development of chronic diseases at older ages should they happen to survive that long. Presumably, smoking and drinking would be most significant in this regard. We are unaware of any data bearing directly on this topic and must leave it simply as a reasonable hypothesis (see, however, Branch and Jette 1984).

To consider the issue of fitness more directly, we compared our sample to one from a noninstitutionalized, more affluent population

Table 3.5. Proportion at Each Age Who Are Independent

Age	Transferring		Dressing		Total No. of Navajos
	Mass. %	Navajos %	Mass. %	Navajos %	
65–69	99.0	100.0	96.0	94.5	73
70–74	96.9	97.4	95.6	97.4	78
75–79	99.4	95.0	95.8	95.0	40
80–84	93.5	97.6	89.6	85.7	42
85 and above	91.7	88.6	83.3	80.0	35

Source: Massachusetts data are from Branch and Fowler 1975.

with higher mortality at old age in Massachusetts (Katz et al. 1983; see also Branch and Fowler 1975, and Branch et al. 1984). The two measures on which we had adequate data were dressing and transfer. Independence in transfer was defined as "moves in and out of bed independently and moves in and out of chair independently (may or may not be using mechanical support)" (Katz and Akpom 1976:496). We have not included data on bathing since the situation for our respondents was not comparable to that for people in Massachusetts with respect to the availability of facilities. Toileting and continence were not included in the Massachusetts data, and due to an oversight on our part, we did not include questions regarding eating.

The differences between Navajos and people of the same age living in Massachusetts were not significant (Table 3.5). Indeed, in their eighties Navajos tended to report slightly lower levels of independence. This, however, may be due to the fact that a higher proportion of the elderly in Massachusetts were in extended care facilities.[6] On the whole, we do not think the crossover phenomenon has resulted in surviving Navajos having dramatically better levels of function than people of the same age in Massachusetts. This is an important issue because it speaks to the debate between those who claim that affluent aging populations include increasing proportions of sick and disabled elderly as life is prolonged, and those who claim that morbidity and disability are avoided as people engage in preventive activities that preserve their health.

Our data suggest that both positions may be correct. If we assume that there are two forms of morbidity—the normal wear and tear of

Table 3.6. Marital Status by Age and Sex

	Men		Women	
Marital Status	Below Age 75	Age 75 and Above	Below Age 75	Age 75 and Above
Married	58	39	38	8
Divorced or separated	5	3	12	3
Widowed	6	10	32	52
Single	2	1	1	1

Comparison	Chi-Square	df	p Value
Men below 75 and 75 and above	3.005	3	.39
Women below 75 and 75 and above	27.735	3	.0001
Men vs. Women	65.27	3	.0001

aging and classifiable nosologic entities—then they may vary independently. Thus, preventive behavior early in life may reduce the risk of severe disease later (e.g., less coronary artery and respiratory disease resulting from less smoking), but not stiff joints, diminished vision, deafness, and the like. These latter causes of diminished function may not be life threatening and may not even require much in the way of acute medical services, but they do make the individual increasingly dependent on some form of help. Whether policymakers and health care providers define them as "medical" problems for which the health care system should assume responsibility is a political and moral decision, not a "scientific" one.

SOCIAL ORGANIZATION AND HEALTH

We turn now to a consideration of the relationship, if any, between social organization and support, on the one hand, and health status and health care utilization on the other. Indicators of health status are scores on the various scales that measure function. In chapters 4 and 5 we deal with the association between nosological entities and social organization.

Table 3.7. Two-way ANOVA: SIP Mean Scores by Age-Sex Group and Marital Status

	Below Age 75		Age 75 and Above	
	Women	Men	Women	Men
Married				
PHYSIP	253	372	566	551
ALBSIP	94	112	203	162
SOISIP	87	92	117	143
TOTSIP	436	577	888	856
Unmarried				
PHYSIP	384	395	656	564
ALBSIP	105	122	177	147
SOISIP	84	132	150	172
TOTSIP	574	671	969	857

ANOVA	Interaction	Age-Sex Group	Marital Status	$Pr > F$
PHYSIP	1.0	.0001	.0201	.0007
ALBSIP	1.0	.008	.38	.088
SOISIP	0.98	.048	.29	.24
TOTSIP	1.0	.0001	.052	.002

Marital Status

Numerous studies have shown that married people tend to have better health and lower mortality than the unmarried. Clearly, it is one of the crucial variables to be taken into account when considering the relationship between social support and health. In our sample men were much less likely to be widowed than women, and younger women were more likely to be married than older women (Table 3.6). There were, however, no differences between younger and older men.

Although a two-way analysis of variance showed, not surprisingly, that age-sex had an effect on the SIP mean scores, marital status had an effect only on PHYSIP (Table 3.7). These significant differences among means, however, are most likely the result of a few extreme values; there were no significant differences among median scores between married and unmarried people in each age-sex group when ordinal rather than interval scales were used (Table 3.8).

Table 3.8. Median Scores of SIP Scales by Age-Sex Group and Marital Status

	Below Age 75		Age 75 and Above	
	Men	*Women*	*Men*	*Women*
Married				
PHYSIP	283	187	418	533
ALBSIP	78	78	78	179
SOISIP	80	52	52	106
TOTSIP	512	379	622	845
Unmarried				
PHYSIP	258	228	350	544
ALBSIP	78	78	123	142
SOISIP	80	36	80	84
TOTSIP	503	342	858	831

Note: The results indicate that there is no significant difference between married and unmarried people within each age-sex group, based on Kruskal-Wallis one-way analysis of variance.

Women under the age of 75 had the lowest rates of hospital utilization and were more likely to be married than older women. We expected that the unmarried women would have higher rates of use than the married because they lacked a crucial source of support and help at home. There was, however, no significant association between marital status and hospital use.[7] Nor was there a significant association between marital status and variables measuring the extensiveness of hospital use among those who were hospitalized.[8] Thus, marital status was not impressively related to either the self-reported level of function or to hospital use with the exception of a few extreme cases among the unmarried, who had significantly higher scores on the PHYSIP scales.

Family and Camp Organization

The Navajo extended family, or camp, is any multihousehold residence group whose households are within shouting distance of each other and cooperate in most subsistence and domestic activities. The preferred type of Navajo residence is the matrilocal camp, composed of a senior parent couple, their unmarried offspring, and one or more

Table 3.9. Camp Type by Community

Community of Residence	Camp Type			
	Neolocal	Matrilocal	Patrilocal	Mixed
Lechee-Coppermine	11	13	1	5
Kaibeto	14	7	3	2
Red Lake	19	12	4	5
Coalmine	8	6	2	1
Gap-Bodaway	6	9	1	4
Tuba City	42	15	7	12
Cameron–Gray Mountain	10	11	0	8

χ^2 = 20.777
df = 18
p = .29

Note: The number of camps is less than the number of informants because in several instances more than one informant resided in a camp.

households formed by this couple's married daughters, their spouses, and dependent children. A patrilocal camp is the same as a matrilocal camp except that it is the sons and their wives who live with the senior parent couple. A neolocal residence is classed as a single-household camp. A mixed camp is comprised of various combinations of matrilocally and patrilocally residing children as well as other kin.

There was no significant difference in the distribution of camp types by community (Table 3.9). In most areas neolocal camps were the single most common type, and matrilocal camps were the most common form of multihousehold camp.[9] Camps of mixed composition were the largest, averaging almost 14 individuals. Matrilocal and patrilocal camps averaged 9 and 9.5, and neolocal camps were the smallest, with an average population of 3.5.

The differences in camp size were reflected in differences in total camp income, which was highest in mixed camps, which averaged about $30,300 a year; lowest in neolocal camps, with about $9,000; and intermediate in the matrilocal and patrilocal camps, which averaged between $16,000 and $19,000. Per capita income, however, was the reverse: neolocal camps were the highest ($3,100), with the other three types essentially identical ($2,200–$2,500).

Wage work provided between 55 and 60 percent of the total income of multihousehold camps. Among neolocal camps, wage work accounted for only 30 percent, with transfer payments (pensions and social security) and unearned income (ADC, SSI, and General Assistance) each providing 30 percent. Unemployment and other sources (livestock and ceremonial earnings) made up the remaining 10 percent. The greater size and wider age spread of the population of multihousehold camps and the greater diversity of sources of income on which they are able to depend account for the different profiles of income by source.

The level of education attained by an individual was related to having had wage work, to having lived off-reservation, and therefore to the availability of retirement benefits, relatively high per capita income, and the presence of running water, electricity, indoor toilets, and motor vehicles in the household (Table 3.10). On the other hand, the characteristics related to education did not include camp size, number of children in the camp, or generational depth. Thus, retirees from steady wage work were not necessarily more likely to live in smaller camps than people who had little or no personal involvement in steady wage work.

The idea that, in a kin-based society, the widowed and divorced would tend to live in an extended family that provided them support during their declining years was not confirmed; neolocal residence was unrelated to marital status (Table 3.11). Nor did we discover any support for the notion that the self-reported level of function would be better in extended families.[10] A higher-than-expected proportion of unmarried men lived in patrilocal camps, and a lower-than-expected proportion lived in matrilocal camps, although why this should be so is not immediately apparent. There was no difference for either men or women in the types of camps in which hospitalized and nonhospitalized people lived, and there was no difference in the mean or median number of years they had lived in their present camps. Finally, we could find no relationship between camp type and any of the variables measuring hospital use among hospitalized respondents.

We thought that people living in small camps would report worse health and more hospital use than people in large camps. Social support is not only thought to exert a positive effect on health but also to be most available in large, multigenerational camps. Presumably there is more manpower available in the large camps to care for sick members so that fewer days would have to be spent in hospital. We used two measures of size: the number of permanent residents and

Table 3.10. Pearson's _r_ Correlation of Individual and Camp Characteristics

	Age	Per Capita Income	Transfer Income	Duration of Steady Job	No. of Vehicles in Camp	Con- veniences[a]	Distance to Tuba City Hosp.	Length of Off- Reservation Steady Wage Work	Number of Permanent Residents in Camp	Number of Children in Camp	Sheep
Women											
Age	—	-.06	-.07	.37b	.06	-.20c	.01	-.38	.08	-.12	-.09
Education	-.36b	.34b	.37b	.42 (=9)	-.01	.44b	-.29c	.77 (=17)	-.13	-.02	-.12
Men											
Age	—	-.01	.05	-.10	-.10	-.20d	.12	-.09	-.01	-.06	0
Education	-.16	.44b	.37b	.51d (=33)	-.01	.20d	-.02	.30d (=83)	-.14	-.01	-.12

[a]Conveniences is a scale which includes type of water source (barrel, cistern, running), working indoor toilet, and electricity
[b]$p = .0001$
[c]$p < .005$
[d]$p < .02$

3.11. Marital Status by Type of Camp

Camp Type	Men		Women	
	Married	Not Married	Married	Not Married
Neolocal	53	11	21	38
Matrilocal	23	4	14	38
Patrilocal	8	5	5	5
Mixed	13	7	6	19

Comparison	χ^2	df	p Value
Married vs. unmarried			
Men	5.74	3	> .05
Women	3.20	3	> .05
All men vs. all women	7.32	3	.06
Men vs. women: married	1.27	3	> .05
Men vs. women: not married	8.93	3	< .05
Total	16.35	9	$\simeq$ .05
Neolocal vs. all other	5.78	3	> .05

the number of children of each respondent living in the camp. The latter is especially significant since children generally assume the major responsibility of caring for their aging parents. Only for the older women was there an inverse relationship between the SIP scores and the number of children and permanent residents in the camp (Tables 3.12 and 3.13). With regard to the older women, it is noteworthy that, for the PHYSIP scores, only the Pearson's r correlation was significant, and barely so at that (p = .053). The Spearman's *rho* correlations were not significant, suggesting the impact of a few extreme cases. With regard to the other SIP scales, Alertness and Social Interaction, the Spearman's *rho* correlations were quite significant. This suggests that the psychosocial functioning of older women is better in large camps, but whether the relationship is causal and, if so, in what direction is moot. Camp size had no effect on whether an individual was hospitalized during the study period.[11]

Associations between camp size, number of children in camp, and hospital use were ambiguous for the group of respondents who had been in hospital. There was a significant positive Pearson's r correlation between the number of children in camp and the number of hos-

Table 3.12. SIP Scores and Number of Permanent Residents in Camp

	PHYSIP	ALBSIP	SOISIP
Women below age 75			
Pearson's r	−.09	−.03	−.19
Spearman's rho	−.09	.007	−.17
Men below age 75			
Pearson's r	−.07	−.10	.02
Spearman's rho	−.09	−.11	−.10
Women age 75 and above			
Pearson's r	−.18	−.26[a]	−.18
Spearman's rho	−.13	−.32[b]	−.21
Men age 75 and above			
Pearson's r	−.07	.03	.04
Spearman's rho	−.07	−.04	−.08

[a] $p = .04$
[b] $p = .01$

pital days for women under age 75 ($p = .03$). This was due, however, to the presence of one alcoholic with active tuberculosis, who lived with several of her children. When she is removed from the analysis, or when rank order correlations are used, the relationships are not significant. Men under 75 from larger camps also spent fewer days in hospital; both Spearman's ($p = .0002$) and Pearson's ($p = .02$) correlations were significant. But this was because, among these men, camp size and PHYSIP were inversely correlated ($r = -.49$). On the other hand, the results of a multiple regression analysis with camp size and PHYSIP as independent variables and number of days in hospital as the dependent variable were insignificant.[12]

Because other studies have shown that the presence of children is important for the elderly and because the range of numbers in our sample was not great, we considered this variable in more detail. Respondents were grouped into those with no children in camp, those with one, and those with two or more. Then, for each age-sex category we did Kruskal-Wallis one-way analyses of variance to compare the number of days in hospital. The results, however, were negative; there were no significant differences in number of hospital days according to the number of children in the camp.

Table 3.13. SIP Scores and Number of Children in Camp

	PHYSIP	ALBSIP	SOISIP
Women below age 75			
Pearson's r	−.10	−.08	−.15
Spearman's rho	−.10	−.06	−.16
Men below age 75			
Pearson's r	−.02	−.09	−.07
Spearman's rho	−.04	−.15	−.10
Women age 75 and above			
Pearson's r	−.24[a]	−.18	−.20
Spearman's rho	−.18	−.20	−.29[b]
Men age 75 and above			
Pearson's r	−.07	.03	.04
Spearman's rho	−.03	.09	.04

[a] $p = .053$
[b] $p = .02$

It is conceivable that these generally unimpressive findings are the result of not controlling for the severity of physical or social dysfunction. We thought that if we considered only people in the top tenth percentile of PHYSIP scores, we would find a higher proportion of individuals who could not be managed at home due to lack of assistance among the 16 people who had been hospitalized than among the 11 who had not. The average number of permanent residents in the camp was 6.9 for the hospitalized group and 7.6 for the nonhospitalized. The former group included two very extreme cases—camps with 18 and 25 members respectively. To test for the significance of the difference between the two groups and to adjust for the impact of extreme cases, we used the Mann-Whitney U test. There was no significant difference between the two groups, so the difference in hospital use among people with extremely high PHYSIP scores cannot be explained by either camp size or number of children in the camp.

Because members of small, neolocal camps had the highest per capita incomes and levels of education, and were also more likely to have running water, electricity, indoor toilets, and motor vehicles, we considered the possibility that our findings were being affected by the level of per capita income. These people were better sheltered from the elements, more able to get to hospital when necessary, and perhaps better able to follow medical advice. Moreover, once hospitalized, the availability of conveniences in the home might be expected to permit them to be discharged after fewer days. Despite these eminently reasonable expectations, however, we found no relationship between self-reported level of functioning and per capita income.[13] Nor were there any significant differences in means and medians of per capita income between hospitalized and nonhospitalized respondents or between per capita income and number of days in hospital.

Finally, we considered the possibility that the socioeconomic variables might have an effect that could not be detected by examining them separately. We combined several of these variables to create a scale of social isolation-integration.[14] The range of possible scores was from 1 to 15, with high scores indicating greater degrees of social contact. The scores were classed as high (10-15 points), medium (5-9), and low (1-4). Proportionately more men than women had high scores, largely because they were more likely to be married.[15] None of the people in the low category was married, all of the high scorers were, and the middle group was split almost evenly.

None of the SIP-scale scores differed among the three social integration categories using Kruskall-Wallis one-way analysis. Nor did a multiple logistic regression using social isolation-integration, PHYSIP, age, sex, and hospital use (yes or no) yield any significant associations except for that between PHYSIP and whether the individual was hospitalized or not. When only those who had been hospitalized were considered, no significant results were obtained for either men or women, suggesting that the increasing availability of relatives in the camp and/or visiting from nearby was not related to fewer days in hospital.[16]

There may be no relationship between social organization and health status and utilization. No one in the study was truly isolated, and in the Navajo context, families may be a burden as well as a support. If this is the case, the quality of the relationships ought to be considered. To examine this more closely, we characterized the children who lived with our respondents as either supportive or not. Those people who lived with impaired children would, we thought, suffer the greatest disability and would use the hospital more than others. The SIP scores and hospital use of the 16 respondents living with an adult child who was mentally ill, retarded, alcoholic, or physically disabled were compared with an equal number of people of the same age and sex but without this characteristic.[17] No significant associations were found by this or a similar analysis comparing the 6 most isolated people with matched controls.

Religion

There is evidence from prospective studies of social support and mortality that church membership is associated with reduced risk of dying in the follow-up period. This is generally attributed to the involvement with others that membership involves. In addition, one study (Zuckerman et al. 1984) found that "religiosity" was also associated with reduced risk of mortality. We considered both dimensions.

In recent decades, nondenominational Christian congregations and revival meetings have become increasingly popular, and Navajos have largely replaced non-Indians as preachers. Membership in the Native American Church (peyotist) appears to have declined as membership in evangelical congregations rose. At the same time, the longer (nine-night) traditional ceremonials, called Sings, have become less and less common because costs are high and people without livestock find it difficult to feed the many guests (Levy and Kunitz 1974). Moreover, the training required to become a ceremonial Singer is long and expensive, and fewer people are able or willing to undertake it. Thus, both across the reservation and in our area the proportion of Singers in the population is diminishing (Aberle 1982; Henderson 1982; Levy 1983).

We classed respondents as Traditional, Native American Church, or Christian if they participated in the activities of one religion to the exclusion of all others, and as Mixed if they participated in any combination of the above. Christians included members of the Church of Jesus Christ of Latter-day Saints (Mormon) as well as the new evangelical Protestant sects and "mainline" Christian churches. No one was exclusively a member of the Native American Church. Those who participated in no religious group whatever were called Irreligious (Table 3.14). There was no significant difference between the religious affiliations of men and women. Over half the people (53 percent) were in the Mixed category, 17 percent were Christian, 29 percent Traditional, and only 1 percent Irreligious.

We thought it possible that people might have converted to Christianity because of physical disability or serious illness. Analyses of covariance with religious affiliation and age as the independent variables and all the SIP scores and measures of hospital utilization as

Table 3.14. Religious Affiliation

Religion	Men	Women
Christian	16	30
Traditional	38	40
Mixed	69	75
Irreligious	1	2
Total	124	147

dependent variables showed that only age was significantly associated with dysfunction and hospital use. Religion was not significant in any instance.

Of course, religious affiliation is not necessarily related to intensity of involvement. To assess this, we used several measures. The first was the number of Sings a respondent had during the five years prior to interview. Since, however, Navajo ceremonial activities are primarily concerned with healing, someone who has been sick might be expected to have more Sings than someone who was in good health, and this may not be a good measure of religious commitment. Men and women classed as Traditional and Mixed did not differ by T-test in the average number of Sings they reported. Several rank-order correlations between the number of Sings and the dependent variables as well as age for men and women separately revealed that for women there was no association between the number of Sings and any of the dependent variables, although older women tended to have had more Sings. For men there was a significant and positive correlation with PHYSIP but not with age. It could well be, of course, that many people who were ill would not have had Sings.

To assess the impact of intensity of religious participation more appropriately, we created a Religious Professional Participation Scale to measure the amount of knowledge commanded by individuals in the sample who were identified as Traditional or mixed Traditional–Native American Church. Low values were assigned to areas of knowledge that were the easiest to learn and that conferred the least ceremonial status. Healing ceremonies were graded by their length as measured by the number of nights it takes to perform the ceremony. Scoring was as follows: Layman with no knowledge = 0; herbal medicine = 1; diagnostician or knowledge of parts of healing ceremonies =

Table 3.15. Rank-Order Correlations of Religious-Professional (Traditional and Traditional/NAC Only) Participation Scale and Dependent Variables

Variables	Men (N = 90)	Women (N = 98)
PHYSIP	.26[a]	.13
ALBSIP	.05	.08
SOISIP	.03	.08
Number of hospitalizations	−.25[a]	.03
Number of hospital days	−.24[b]	.05
Number of tests	−.23[b]	.05
Number of operations	−.21[c]	.01
Age	.25[a]	.22[c]

[a]$p = .01$
[b]$p = .02$
[c]$p = .04$

2; three-night healing ceremony = 3; five-night healing ceremony = 4; nine-night healing ceremony = 5.

Ninety men received scores ranging from 0 to 25. The mean was 3.8. The highest-scoring individual, for example, was a man who knew one nine-night ceremony (5 points); four five-night ceremonies (16 points); hand trembling diagnosing (2 points); and some parts of ceremonies (2 points). His total score was 25 points.

Women were scored in the same manner, with one exception. None of the women were ceremonialists, but two had learned whole ceremonies, although they did not perform them. We scored them as if they did because the knowledge required was equal to that required of a male ceremonialist. The range of scores was much less for the women: 98 received scores ranging from 0 to 9. The mean was 1.01, and the median 0. Forty-eight women (49 percent) had knowledge of herbal medicine, and 28 knew hand trembling.

Older men and women had more ceremonial knowledge. PHYSIP was correlated both with age and the scale, so age is probably a confounding variable; older men had more ceremonial knowledge and were also more likely to suffer physical dysfunction (Table 3.15). For women, however, there were no significant associations between the scale and the dependent variables, perhaps because the range of women's scores on the scale was very small and thus did not adequately distinguish among them. For men, but not for women, the greater the level of ceremonial knowledge, the lower the level of hospital use.

To assess the relation between ceremonial knowledge and the dependent variables more fully, we compared the 24 ceremonialists (men who knew at least one three-night Sing) to controls matched for age and sex using the Wilcoxon signed ranks test. The ceremonialists had significantly higher levels of physical dysfunction (PHYSIP) and some tendency, approaching significance, to spend fewer days in hospital.[18]

The reasons for men who were most involved in traditional religion to report the worst physical function but to spend fewer days in hospital are not entirely clear. Based on our long acquaintance with Crooked Finger and Falconer, however, we think it has something to do with the fact that these Singers were very active, and made great demands on themselves well into old age. Because they were so active, they were aware of many aches and pains. They were reluctant to use hospitals, however, because they viewed modern medicine and most physicians as antagonistic to traditional Navajo religion, as indeed they were during the years these men were most active.

To measure the impact of adherence to Christianity on health status, we divided people into exclusive, active, and occasional Christians. Since there were only 51 people in all three groups combined, we have considered men and women together. Exclusive Christians attended church frequently and never participated in any other religious ceremonies. Active Christians attended church frequently and occasionally attended traditional or Native American Church ceremonies. Occasional Christians attended church infrequently but did not attend other religious ceremonies. We compared SIP scores among the three groups using analysis of variance and found no significant differences among them. Thus, intensity of involvement with Christian churches is unrelated to health status.

Lastly we compared SIP scores of all those who claimed some religious affiliation with those of people who claimed none. Again there were no differences. Thus, if religiosity does not bring measurable health benefits, at least it seems to cause no discernible harm.

CONCLUSION

With but one notable exception, the associations between our measures of health and those of social organization, income, and religion were nonexistent. Camp size and the number of coresident children were each associated with the psychosocial functioning of women 75 years of age and above. There were no associations with level of physical functioning or with hospital use, however, which suggests that physical functioning is largely unrelated to social organization or income (always keeping in mind that maximum income is low and range of income narrow in this population). But if psychological status and social functioning are importantly related to domestic organization, at least in one segment of the population, the causal associations are still unclear. Nevertheless, some disorders are thought by many to be directly influenced by environmental stress, and it is to a consideration of two of these, depression and hypertension, that we turn in succeeding chapters.

▸▸ 4 ◂◂

DEPRESSION

DEPRESSION IS THOUGHT by many to be sensitive to the social environment, often precipitated by stressful life events and exacerbated by social isolation, poor health, and low economic status. Its distribution among elderly Navajos ought, then, to reveal whether the role played by kinship ties is a protective one. The cultural distinctiveness of the Navajos, however, raises the question of whether culture itself is an important factor in determining the prevalence and expression of psychiatric disorders (Fabrega 1974; Marsella 1978). Most studies of depression in non-Western societies have reported very low prevalence rates or have questioned the universality of the disorder itself, pointing out that the concept of depression is totally lacking in many societies and that several of its key symptoms are not found in many parts of the world (Marsella 1980). These studies suggest that depression may be either absent or very infrequent among elderly Navajos if they lack the concept of depression as a disease category or have a tendency to manifest the disorder more through somatic than affective symptoms (Katon et al. 1982). On the other hand, depression is said to be the most frequently diagnosed problem among American Indians presenting for treatment at mental health facilities, and some have speculated that its prevalence may be four to six times higher in Indian communities than in the general population (Manson et al. 1985:332). Cross-cultural studies of depression, however, exhibit the same flaws that have plagued studies of the general population, and although the quantity and quality of epidemiological research on psychiatric disorders have increased dramatically over the past thirty years, interpreting the results has been made difficult by the lack of comparability between studies that have used a great variety of definitions and measures of depression and that have been conducted among hospitalized patients as well as the general population (Weissman and Klerman 1978).

Most epidemiological studies of depression in the community measure the prevalence of self-reported symptoms rather than making direct diagnoses. A simple measure of symptom frequency cannot discriminate between clinical depression, such conditions as bereavement and adjustment reaction with depression, which are not considered pathological, and fortuitous combinations of somatic and affective symptoms. In consequence, the proportion of falsely identified cases is unknown. The procedure, however, has been justified by claiming that a "significant" level of symptomatology indicates the need for therapeutic intervention, suggesting in effect that a depression scale score can be used effectively as a case screening device. Because we could not assume that the magnitude of the difference between the prevalence of clinical depression and that of significant symptomatology as defined by a scale score was the same for Navajos and the general population, we used both methods.

In recent years, community epidemiological studies have increasingly utilized a self-reported symptom checklist in conjunction with a set of operational criteria for psychiatric diagnosis established by the most recent edition of the *Diagnostic and Statistical Manual for Psychiatric Disorders* (*DSM* III) and with any of several measures of physical and cognitive dysfunction. Our original intent was to use the Diagnostic Interview Schedule for Depression (DIS-D) recently developed by the National Institute of Mental Health (Robins, Helzer, Croughan, Williams, and Spitzer 1981; Robins, Helzer, Croughan, and Ratcliff 1981).

The DIS is a fully structured interview designed to enable physicians and nonphysicians to make consistent and accurate psychiatric diagnoses in patients and the general population according to three diagnostic systems: the *DSM* III, the Feighner criteria, and the Research Diagnostic Criteria (RDC). After encountering several difficulties during pretesting in the summer of 1981, however, several modifications were made that resulted in a shortened format designed to be incorporated into the larger interview without making the entire instrument unwieldy. The highly structured format was abandoned

doned because respondents considered it too repetitious. Whether because Navajos do not organize their lives around time as measured by clocks and calendars or because the symptoms actually varied widely in duration and periodicity, the repeated questions demanding precision in this regard were difficult for the Navajos to answer. More satisfactory results were obtained by allowing respondents to recount their experiences in their own way before the interviewer probed to determine duration, intensity, periodicity, and coexistence of symptoms or other conditions that might affect the diagnosis.

The DIS-D identifies 18 symptoms. Our shortened list contained only 12 of these (Table 4.1). Several items were already included in the SIP sections of the interview, while others, such as loss of interest in sex, thoughts of death, and moving more slowly, did not have much salience in an elderly population. Sleeping too much was mentioned spontaneously in the narratives, and although it was used for diagnostic purposes, it was not coded as part of the depression scale. The item about guilt feelings was rephrased because respondents had a very negative reaction to the question and often wished to terminate the interview if the interviewer persisted in asking.

For each of the 12 items, a score of 0 was given if the symptom was entirely absent or had been present for only a day or two at a time and the episodes did not recur with any frequency. A score of 1 was given if the symptom persisted for more than a few days at a time but did not recur with any frequency. A score of 2 was given for acute symptoms that persisted for two or more weeks even though, as was most often the case, there were symptom-free periods of from one to five days. The maximum score possible was 24. Six of the items referred to somatic and 6 to affective symptoms. Eleven of the 18 symptoms in the original DIS-D list referred to somatic complaints. By contrast, only 4 of the 20 items in the widely used Center for Epidemiological Studies Depression Scale (CES-D) represented somatic symptoms (Radloff 1977). We believed that decreasing the proportion of somatic symptoms was appropriate because, among the elderly, many somatic symptoms of depression may be consequent on actual physical illness so that depression scales that weigh physical symptoms heavily may result in inflated estimates. On the other hand, clinicians are likely to overlook somatic complaints that might indicate the presence of depression (Blazer and Williams 1980; Weiss et al. 1986). Following the majority of studies that utilize symptom scale scores to identify depression, a score of about one-third the maximum possible—in our

Table 4.1. Symptom List from the DIS-D

Navajo List	Original DIS-D List
A. Psychological	
1. Periods of depression during past year.	1. Depressed, loss of interest or pleasure for two or more weeks.
2. Recurrent depression past 2 years.	2. Depressed most of the time for 2 years.
3. Feels useless and a burden.	3. Feels worthless, sinful, guilty.
4. Life not worth living and/or thoughts of death.	4. Thoughts of death.
	5. Wanted to die.
5. Suicidal ideation.	6. Suicidal ideation.
6. Suicide attempt.	7. Suicide attempt.
B. Somatic	
7. Difficulty making decisions and plans or learning new things.	8. Trouble concentrating.
	9. Thoughts come slower.
8. Loss of appetite.	10. Loss of appetite.
9. Loss of weight.	11. Loss of weight.
	12. Weight gain due to increased appetite.
10. Insomnia, sleeping difficulties.	13. Insomnia.
	14. Sleeping too much.
11. Fatigue.	15. Fatigue.
	16. Talked or moved more slowly.
12. Restlessness.	17. Restlessness.
	18. Loss of interest in sex.

case a score of 9 or above—was used as the cut-off point indicating the probable existence of clinical depression (Ensel 1982; Zung 1965).

Diagnoses according to *DSM* III were made by reviewing the entire interview form, the interviewer's observations, and the respondent's narrative accounts in the depression and other health sections. Together, these materials provided enough information on medical problems, drug use, and major psychiatric or cognitive disorders to permit a tentative diagnosis. Clinical depressions were coded as major depression, dysthymic disorder (minor depression), and atypical depression. No cases of either bipolar or cyclothymic disorder were found. Two normal conditions—bereavement and adjustment reaction—were coded if the associated symptoms of depression were acute and had persisted for three or more months. These latter conditions, however, were not included in the category "clinical depression."

There was no bias due to differences among either interviewers or interpreters, and a separate review of the medical charts identified no cases of depression not already identified by the field procedure. Nor were any cases diagnosed by this method shown to be false by evidence contained in the medical charts. In fact, quite the reverse was true. Of the 26 individuals classified as clinically depressed, only three had been diagnosed in hospital during the 1980–1983 period. But because depression is often mentioned in the charts without a diagnosis having been coded, the inclusion of all chart notations, even those for previous years, is a more instructive calculation. In all, nine individuals had some mention made of their depression in the charts. Four of these were dated prior to 1980.

PREVALENCE OF DEPRESSION AND ITS SYMPTOMS

Two community studies have estimated point prevalence rates of depression among the elderly using *DSM* III criteria. In New Haven, Connecticut, a rate of 10 percent was reported by Weissman and Myers (1979, 1980). In Durham County, North Carolina, the rate was 8.2 (Blazer and Williams 1980). We were unable to estimate point prevalence rates with any degree of confidence because our Navajo respondents always insisted they had gotten better during the week or month prior to the interview despite the fact that many exhibited observable signs of depression during the interview. We calculated a one-year prevalence rate of 9.6 and a one-month prevalence rate of 8.1.

Studies of the elderly using the CES-D depression scale report point prevalence rates for probable depression between 14.8 percent in a national sample (Eaton and Kessler 1981) and 16.5 percent in Kentucky (Murrell et al. 1983). The one-year prevalence rate for the Navajos using the symptom scale scores was 18.5 percent. Given the transient nature of symptoms, we do not think this rate indicates a significant difference, however.

Cultural variables and socioeconomic status are both said to influence the reporting if not the actual experiencing of the various symptoms of depression (Marsella 1980; Crandell and Dohrenwend 1967). Poor ethnic minorities and many non-Western societies are said to have a tendency to somatize. That is, they report the physiological symptoms of depression more often than the psychological. In addition, people in many non-Western societies are said not to experience feelings of self-deprecation, guilt, or suicidal impulses, and some are said hardly to experience dysphoria at all. Much of what is known about Navajo culture would lead us to expect that Navajos' responses to the symptom lists would be very different from those of the general population. Navajo culture has been described as shame rather than guilt oriented (Leighton and Kluckhohn 1947; Piers and Singer 1953), and age-specific suicide rates for Navajos over age 65 are low (Levy 1965; Kunitz 1983).

To the extent that the various depression scale items are similar across studies, we can compare the mean scores for each symptom expressed as a percent of the maximum score possible on each item with the prevalence of each symptom in the study population (Table 4.2). Two facts impress themselves at the outset: Navajo respondents did not report physiological symptoms more than psychological ones, and there was nothing to suggest that any specific symptoms were either absent or of little salience. Suicidal ideation and attempts were the least frequently reported items among Navajos and non-Navajos alike. Twice as many Navajos reported dysphoria as did the elderly in the general population. The PERI scale asks whether suicide was ever attempted, yet the scores for this item were somewhat lower among the rural women to whom this scale was administered than among the Navajos who reported for the previous year only (Newman 1984).

The depressed patients interviewed by Zung (1965) had higher mean scores generally but especially for suicidal ideation than did the Navajos diagnosed as depressed. The non-Indian patients were younger than the Navajos and had been hospitalized with acute complaints. Most of them probably suffered from major depression. This, we believe, would account for their higher scores, because most of the depressed Navajos (77 percent) suffered from dysthymic disorder (i.e., minor depression), which tends to be less acute. It is noteworthy that

Table 4.2. Symptom Intensity (Mean Score in Percent) and Prevalence (in Percent)

| | Mean score | | | | Prevalence | |
| | Clinically Depressed Patients | | Rural[b] | | | |
Symptoms	Navajo 65+ (N = 25)	Non-Indian[a] adult (N = 31)	Navajo 65+ (N = 269)	Women adult (N = 542)	Navajo 65+ (N = 269)	General Population[c] 65+ (N = Unknown)
A. Physiological						
Insomnia	78%	87%	40%		44%	43%
Fatigue	64	87	27		31	30[d]
Appetite loss	50	73	23		27	19
Restlessness	30	73	13		15	
Difficulty making decisions	16	73	11		15	
Weight loss	20	67	11		11	
B. Psychological						
Depressed past year	86	73	42	34.5%[e]	48	20
2 yr. recurrent depression	76		30		35	
Useless and a burden	46	50	22	13.7[f]	26	
Thoughts of death, or life not worth living	46	66[g]	12	11.0[h]	12	
Suicidal ideation	20	63	5	1.0	5	
Suicide attempt	8		1	1.7[i]	2	

Note: Navajo data are based on one-year prevalence. All other studies are based on point prevalence, with the sole exception of one item on the PERI scale, which asks whether suicide has *ever* been attempted.
[a]*Source:* Zung (1965) SDS.
[b]*Source:* Newman (1984) PERI.
[c]*Source:* Craig and Van Natta (1983) CES-D.
[d]Can't get going.
[e]Feelings of sadness or depression.
[f]Feeling bad or worthless.
[g]Hopelessness.
[h]Hopeless about everything.
[i]Suicide attempt ever.

the clinically depressed Navajos scored higher on the depression items and generally lower on all somatic items than did the hospitalized non-Indian patients despite the Navajos' advanced age, with its attendant physical disabilities, suggesting that somatization may not be as significant as is usually thought.

PHYSICAL WELLBEING

Significant associations between depression and self-reported physical disability were found by studies using the CES-D (Craig and Van Natta 1983; Frerichs et al. 1982; Murrell et al. 1983). The best predictor of depression among the elderly in Kentucky was a measure of overall physical health. Craig and Van Natta also found a significant association with various measures of hospital use. All of these studies found that the correlations held for both sexes, although women reported more depression than men.

Among the Navajos there was no correlation between diagnosed depression and any of the sickness impact (SIP) scales. High depression scale scores, however, were positively associated with the mobility scale (MOBSIP) but only among women under 75 years of age (Pearson's correlation coefficient, $p < .01$). For women over 75 and for men, there was no association between depression scale scores and the PHYSIP scales. The p values were, in fact, impressive only because they approached 1.0 in most instances.

The social interaction (SOISIP) and alertness behavior (ALBSIP) scales were positively associated with depression scale scores— ALBSIP among all except males over 75 and SOISIP among males under 75 and women over 75. We believe these associations reflect nothing more than the tendency for depressed people to be socially withdrawn and to experience difficulty concentrating.

There was no difference in depression scores between those who were and were not hospitalized (using Kruskal-Wallis analysis of variance). Among the hospitalized, however, both Pearson's and Spearman's correlation coefficients showed significant correlations with extensiveness of hospital use except for males 75 and older.

As we report in chapter 3, the people in our sample with the longest hospital stays and the most serious illnesses are below the age of 75. Those above that age who reported high levels of disability on the SIP scales suffered from such problems as reduced vision, osteoarthritis, deafness, and the like, but they did not have conditions such as respiratory failure and renal failure, which are found among a few younger people in the sample. There was no correlation between high depression scores and any of the life-threatening diseases. The only positive association was with alcoholism. In fact, all the males diagnosed as clinically depressed were also very heavy drinkers.

Age

The prevalence of symptoms increases after age 75 for both males and females in the general population (Eaton and Kessler 1981; Murrell et al. 1983). Depression scores were not correlated with age among either men or women in our sample, and mean depression scores of men were essentially the same in the two age groups ($<$ 75 = 15.2 percent; $\geq$ 75 = 14.8 percent). The women's scores, however, declined with age ($<$ 75 = 22.7 percent; $\geq$ 75 = 18.2 percent).

Blazer and Williams (1980) found that the point prevalence rate for major depression remained stable but that minor depression, which was 5.4 percent for both sexes between age 65 and 74, declined to 2.5 percent after age 75. The Navajo period prevalence rates for both major and minor depression remained stable.

Sex

In an adult population of all ages, twice as many women as men scored at or above the "caseness" cut-off point on the CES-D scale (Eaton and Kessler 1981). In elderly populations, however, between 1.33 and 1.28 women to each male scored in this range (Ensel 1982; Murrell et al. 1983). Among the elderly Navajos, the female-to-male ratio was 2.3 : 1.

For diagnosed depressions, Weissman and Myers (1979) report that differences in the point prevalence rates disappear after age 65. Rates for the elderly in Durham County were: (a) minor depression: males, 3.8 percent; females, 5.0 percent; (b) major depression: males, 3.2 percent; females 4.0 percent (Murrell et al. 1983). One-month prevalence rates for the Navajos were: (a) minor depression: males, 3.2 percent; females, 11.0 percent; (b) major depression: males, 0.0 percent; females, 1.4 percent. In addition, 0.7 percent of females had atypical depression.

It is not clear, given the small number of Navajos, whether the differences between the two populations are significant or males were underdiagnosed because of the prevalence of drinking among Navajo men (Levy and Kunitz 1974).

All of the men diagnosed as depressed in our sample had histories of heavy drinking going back 20 to 40 years. In each case the information required to make an adequate diagnosis was provided by the wife because these men were extremely reticent about their affective symptoms. There was one man who had been diagnosed in hospital as chronically depressed in years past but whose drinking resulted in a chronic brain syndrome that made diagnosing depression impossible at the time of the interview. One wife believed that her husband only became depressed and suicidal while drinking, but because the drinking started only after the death of a favorite son, it is more likely that it was a response to depression rather than its cause. We think that several cases of depression among males have been missed due to the masking effect of drinking, but it is also possible that men who drink excessively tend to die earlier than more moderate drinkers so that both underreporting and higher mortality may account for the low proportion of clinically depressed males. Consistent with these findings regarding clinical depression, women scored higher than men on the scale of symptoms associated with depression (using Kruskal-Wallis analysis of variance: $p < 0.01$).

MARITAL STATUS

Higher rates of depression are frequently found among the widowed, separated, or divorced than among married people (Weissman and Klerman 1977; Weissman and Myers 1979; Blazer and Williams 1980; Murphy 1982; Roberts and Vernon 1982). Among the Navajos neither clinical depression nor high depression scores were associated with marital status. For example, within each age-sex category there was no difference between married and unmarried respondents with respect to depression scores except among women under age 75 (using Kruskal-Wallis analysis of variance). Thus, with age and sex controlled, marital status is unrelated to symptoms usually associated with depression (see Table 4.3). A possible explanation of this unexpected finding, to be explored more fully below, is that the extended family and supportive kin network so prevalent among the Navajos

Table 4.3. Navajo Depression Scale Scores by Age, Sex, and Marital Status

	N	*Mean Score*
Men below age 75		
Married	57	15.1%
Not married	13	15.7
Men age 75 and above		
Married	39	13.7
Not married	14	17.8
Women below age 75		
Married	38	18.3
Not married	45	26.4
Women age 75 and above		
Married	8	17.2
Not Married	55	17.9

Analysis of covariance (dependent variable is the depression score)			
Age/sex	df = 3	F = 2.77	p = .0415
Marital status	df = 1	F = 4.94	p = .0271
Age/sex/marital status	df = 3	F = 0.0	p = 1.0

may protect the widowed, divorced, and separated from developing severe depression.

SOCIOECONOMIC STATUS

Strong inverse correlations between the markers of economic position (income, education, home ownership, employment status) have been found by a number of community studies (Uhlenhuth et al. 1974; Wahrheit et al. 1973; Brown et al. 1975; Comstock and Helsing 1976; Murphy 1982; Murrell et al. 1983). None of the measures of economic wellbeing were associated with depression among the Navajos, however. Because the Navajos in our sample clustered at the lower end of the economic spectrum and their educational level was also low, it is possible that the range of variability was too small to yield the expected results. In addition, the effects of income and education on depres-

Table 4.4. Social Isolation and Clinical Depression

	Clinical Depression				
	Present		Absent		
Social Isolation Score	Observed	Expected	Observed	Expected	Total
Men					
Low	0	(0.4)	15	(14.6)	15
Medium	1	(1.1)	42	(41.9)	43
High	2	(1.5)	59	(59.5)	61
Total	3		116		119

$\chi^2 = 0.591$; df = 2; $p > .7$

	Clinical Depression				
Women					
Low	6	(2.75)	13	(16.25)	19
Medium	9	(13.04)	81	(76.96)	90
High	5	(4.2)	24	(24.3)	29
Total	20		118		138

$\chi^2 = 6.133$; df = 2; $p < .05$

sion are attenuated in rural areas (Eaton and Kessler 1981). If this is the case, however, one would expect to find a higher prevalence of depression than we did due to the generally harsh conditions of reservation life—unless, of course, the Navajos in our sample are healthier than their age mates in the general population. There is no evidence to support this, as we indicate in chapter 3.

SOCIAL ISOLATION

Strong social support networks are said to protect against depression and reduce the intensity of depressive symptoms (Murphy 1982; Dunkle 1983; Lin and Ensel 1984; Norris and Murrell 1984; Lin et al. 1985). We have already had occasion to note that marital status may not be a strong predictor of depression among Navajos because the social support provided by the extended family and large kin networks would lessen the effects of losing a spouse. The Social Isolation–Inte-

Table 4.5. Residence with Own Children

| | Children Present in Camp | | | | | | | | |
| | Daughters | | Both Sons and Daughters | | Sons | | None | | |
	Observed	Expected	Observed	Expected	Observed	Expected	Observed	Expected	Total
Men	27	(44.8)	23	(18.7)	27	(21.5)	49	(41.1)	126
Women	69	(51.2)	17	(21.3)	19	(24.5)	39	(46.9)	144
Total	96		40		46		88		270

$\chi^2 = 20.682$; df = 3; $p = .001$

gration Scale, we thought, might be a better predictor of depression than marital status.

Chi-square analysis revealed no association between the level of social isolation and diagnosed depression for men, although there was a significant difference for women (Table 4.4). When compared using Kruskal-Wallis analysis of variance, depression scores varied significantly by level of social isolation for men and women. People in the lowest category on the social isolation scale (most isolated) had the highest depression scale scores, whereas people in the highest category (least isolated) had the lowest scores. When we considered the components of the social isolation scale in addition to marital status, only number of people in the camp proved important. Those who lived with more than one other person had significantly lower depression scores than those who lived with only one other person (no one lived permanently in a single-person camp).

The presence or absence of one or more of the respondent's own children in the camp was not associated with responses to the depression symptom scale. We have suggested that extended families may be burdensome as well as supportive. These results—or nonresults— may point in that direction. To examine this possibility further, we selected all those people who lived with an adult child who was mentally ill, retarded, alcoholic, or physically disabled ($N = 16$) and compared them with a set of controls matched for age and sex. Although there were no differences between the two groups with respect to the health and hospital use measures, those who lived with impaired children had significantly higher depression scale scores than did the controls ($p < .025$). These findings suggest that while

Table 4.6. Clinical Depression Among Women and Presence of Children in Camp

| | Children Present in Camp | | |
	Daughters	Sons Only or None	Total
Depressed	8	14	22
Not depressed	78	44	122
Total	86	58	144

$\chi^2 = 5.8$; df = 1; $p < .02$

being isolated may be associated with depression, as either cause or effect, the simple fact of living with others does not adequately capture the quality of relationships. Much depends on the reasons for coresidence.

But the issue is even more complicated. The ideal Navajo extended family is based on matrilocal residence and matrilineal descent, which creates a domestic group, or camp, comprised of a parent couple, their unmarried children, and their married daughters with their husbands and unmarried children. This suggests that the bonds between mothers and their daughters may be more important emotionally than those between mothers and sons and that, in consequence, older women not living with their daughters may be more at risk for depression than those who live with their sons or with other relatives.

Men lived with their daughters less frequently than did women (Table 4.5). While there were too few depressed men to yield any meaningful correlations, all of the clinically depressed men (4) were living with their wives in their own camps, and three of these had their own daughters living with them. We do not take this to mean either that the father-daughter or the marital bond promotes depression. The information required to make the diagnosis of depression was provided by these men's wives, indicating only that depression may be underreported among males who were not living with their wives and daughters because men are very reluctant to talk about depression.

In sharp contrast to the men, significantly fewer Navajo women were clinically depressed if they lived with a daughter (Table 4.6). But because the depression scale scores were not lower among women who lived with their daughters, it is important to explore this finding

Table 4.7. Women's Depression and the Rearing of Daughters

| | Whether Reared Daughters | | |
Clinical Depression	Yes	No	Total
Present	18	4	22
Absent	116	6	122
Total	134	10	144

$\chi^2 = 5.26$

$df = 1$

$p \approx .02$

further and to ask whether the mother-daughter bond protects against depression or the depression alienates daughters.

Although similar proportions of depressed and nondepressed women had borne no children at all, had borne only sons, or had children who died in childhood, the childless, nondepressed women had adopted or raised one or more of their sisters' children so that significantly more depressed women had never raised a daughter (Table 4.7).

Among the depressed women was one who never married and never had children because she was slightly retarded. She lived with her mother and older sister and became chronically depressed only after her mother died at an advanced age. A major depression was precipitated a year later by the death of her older sister. Another childless depressed woman was characterized as having a difficult personality. She was married for three months as a young woman and never repeated the experiment. These were the only women in the sample who had not really been married.

Eighteen depressed women had raised daughters, but only eight were living with a daughter at the time of the interview. Four of the women living with a daughter and two who were not had been so difficult to live with that the daughters felt alienated. Four women said they did not live with their daughters because their depression became more acute when they were together. These respondents said they liked their daughters and that there was no friction in their relationships. Rather, they felt increasingly worthless and desirous of solitude when with them. In all, ten of the eighteen depressed women who had raised daughters had defective relationships with them.

Without an evaluation of mother-daughter relationships among the nondepressed women and more detailed family histories, the interpretation of these findings must remain tentative.

The effect of isolation on the prevalence of symptoms associated with depression is obscured by a number of factors—the presence of impaired adult children in the camp who are dependent on their elderly parents, for example—that make living in an extended family less supportive than it may be in the general population. Clinical depression, on the other hand, appears to exert an influence on living arrangements rather than being caused by them. Clinically depressed women often had preexisting psychological conditions that precluded their marrying and either bearing or raising children with whom they could live in later life. They also tended to alienate their daughters or to prefer living away from them.

STRESS AT THE COMMUNITY LEVEL

There is some question whether the prevalence of psychiatric symptoms is elevated in communities experiencing stress. A portion of the area in which we worked falls within what is called the Joint Use Area (JUA), a tract of land that has been partitioned between the Hopi and Navajo tribes. In the 1930s the federal government took half the Hopi Indian Reservation, which since the nineteenth century had been settled by many Navajos, and made it part of the surrounding Navajo Reservation. The Hopi Tribe protested this action, and in the 1950s a federal court ruled that the area was to be used jointly by the two tribes. Sharing the royalties derived from the large coal deposits presented few problems, but the question of how the land was to be used became, over the years, a political issue of vexing proportions. The federal court ruled that the surface area was to be partitioned equally between the two tribes and that, until the boundaries could be agreed upon, livestock holdings of Navajos living in the JUA would have to be reduced. Ultimately the lines were drawn, and Navajo families living in the area assigned to the Hopis were encouraged to relocate. It is important to note that the elderly were not asked to leave. Nevertheless, stock reduction, a moratorium on all construction, and the general political climate were such that even the older Navajos were considerably affected. Respondents living in the JUA were quite vocal in expressing their dissatisfaction with the restrictions placed upon

Table 4.8. Number of Traditional Ceremonies During the Past Year

| | No. of Ceremonies | | | | | | |
| | 0 | | 1 | | 2 or more | | |
	Observed	Expected	Observed	Expected	Observed	Expected	Total
Depressed	9	(10)	3	(6.2)	7	(2.8)	19
Not depressed	107	(106)	69	(65.8)	25	(29.2)	201
Total	116		72		32		220[a]

$\chi^2 = 8.82$
df = 2
$p < .01$

[a]Not involved in traditional religion: 50 (depressed, 6; not depressed, 44)

them. Worry about the future was a prominent feature of many of the interviews. Whether, as some Navajo leaders have claimed, there was also a measurable increase in the prevalence of psychiatric disorders is a question amenable to empirical investigation.

Of the 263 respondents for whom we had data, 59 lived in or had recently moved from the JUA. Nine had left the Navajo section, while another 32 still lived there. Six had left the area assigned to the Hopis, while 12 remained. None of the relocatees was clinically depressed, although 4 had depression scale scores above the cut-off point. By neither measure was depression overrepresented in the JUA group.

TREATMENT

Depending on how the question is put, between 35 and 50 percent of all adults diagnosed as depressed seek treatment for emotional or family problems during the year prior to interview (Weissman and Myers 1980; Roberts and Vernon 1982; Wing and Bebbington 1982). Among the elderly, however, only 8 percent had sought help from any professional, including ministers and nonpsychiatric nurses (Weissman and Myers 1979), and only 3.4 percent admitted having needed help for mental problems (Murrell et al. 1983).

The Navajo sample did not appear to differ appreciably in this respect. Two clinically depressed Navajos (7.7 percent) had sought help from the hospital specifically for their depression during the year prior to interview. Two others had had traditional Navajo ceremonial treatments, one specifically for the symptoms of major depression, the other for the events that had precipitated a major depression. Most often, depressed Navajos sought treatment for conditions other than depression. Three were seen by physicians who, while noting the presence of dysphoria in the chart, made no diagnosis and treated only the presenting problem. Similarly, six others had traditional ceremonies during the year for complaints other than depression. Among those respondents who were involved in the traditional religion, the clinically depressed averaged more ceremonies during the year (1.0) than did those who were not depressed (0.66), and the difference between the two groups was significant (Table 4.8).

CONCLUSION

Depression, then, seems to be about as prevalent among Navajos as it is in the population generally. Considering that this has often been assumed not to be the case, the absence of a difference is itself significant. It is also important to point out that the two ways of measuring depression, by using either a symptom checklist or a wide range of questions to make a clinical diagnosis, generally but not invariably give similar results. Symptoms, however, tend to be responsive to situational factors, whereas clinical diagnosis is based on symptoms as well as other sources of information, which tend to reflect long-term patterns of behavior and effect as well. Thus, almost by definition, they are less situationally specific than symptoms; they may reflect lifelong styles of relating to others, and they may themselves be independent variables that may help to explain contemporary living arrangements.

This is an important distinction because, depending on which method is chosen, one may come to very different conclusions about cause and effect. We believe that clinical depression may well result from social isolation, but our evidence also suggests that the converse is at least as important: depression over a long period seems to result in increasing social isolation. Symptoms, on the other hand, seem to be responsive to social situations and thus may be more usefully considered effects rather than causes.

These observations pertain more to women than to men. Among

the latter, depression is more difficult to assess because alcohol use often obscures it. Previously we have shown that heavy drinking is common among young men and that most of them stop or moderate their drinking as they enter early middle age but that a small number continue heavy drinking and go on to become chronic alcoholics (Levy and Kunitz 1974). We do not know why this happens, and the present study was not designed to investigate the question. Among some of them, continued drinking probably is a means of coping with long-term depression. Since the data on depression often come from wives of men who drink a lot, however, unmarried men who drink would be underrepresented among the men we have labeled clinically depressed. This is a significant potential bias and may be reflected in findings presented in chapter 7, that men at the highest risk of dying during the period of follow-up tend to be unmarried and to have histories of heavy alcohol consumption.

Overall, our findings suggest that depression among the Navajos is not much different from that in the general population. Cultural differences, rather than affecting the prevalence or manifestation of depression, appear to affect the utility of the measures of the factors believed to cause or aggravate it. Size of residence groups, for example, does not measure social support as accurately in a kin-based society, in which survival depends on coresidence, as it may in a society in which living with relatives is more a matter of personal choice. Similarly, the importance of marital status is obscured in societies in which the loss of a spouse does not lead to social isolation as often as it does in the general population. The effects of income and education on depression are attenuated in rural areas of the nation generally but are obscured entirely among the Navajos, among whom education levels are low and the range of incomes is small.

The various measures of physical wellbeing were also found to be less predictive of depression among the Navajos than in the general population. Individuals over age 75 appear to suffer less from life-threatening illness than do those under that age. Thus, levels of self-reported disability in the two age groups measure two different classes of phenomena without distinguishing between them so that the relationship between ill health and depression tends to be obscured. Differences in health status and mortality affect the applicability of the indicators, not the characteristics of depression.

A typical view of the area around Tuba City. The vistas are vast and dramatic, but walking on sand is difficult, and managing a wheelchair in this terrain is almost impossible.

The forked-stick hogan is the most ancient form of Navajo dwelling. Although fewer and fewer are seen on the reservation today, many of the elderly in the western part of the reservation still prefer them. The seventy-eight-year-old retired ceremonialist and his wife who live in this hogan are seventeen miles from a hospital and nine miles from a paved road.

The forked-stick hogan's log and mud construction provides good insulation so that it is cool in the summer and relatively easy to heat in winter with a wood-burning stove made from a fifty-gallon oil drum. Space is limited, however, and storage is often a problem.

Hogans with cribbed "beehive" log roofs and upright log walls are more common and enclose more space while still retaining the advantages of the circular floor plan for heating and cooling. In this room there is ample room for a loom. Fabric has been nailed to the roof logs to prevent mud and insects from falling through the chinks between the logs.

In recent years, more and more hogans have been built with modern materials. These homes are usually larger than the average log hogan and have windows that provide more light. They are also easier to keep clean, as floors are often of plywood covered with linoleum. The thin walls provide poor insulation, however, so that they are harder to heat and cool.

This simple shed provides a separate area for a portable toilet that faces away from the areas of most activity.

Innumerable combinations of traditional and modern forms are possible. In this hogan the upright walls are provided with windows, while the dirt floor and cribbed log roof are retained. Large sheets of plastic have been placed over the mud-covered roof to retard erosion. Eight people live in this one-room dwelling.

This widow of a famous ceremonialist lives in a large camp that includes three houses, three trailers, and two hogans. Although the houses have running water and indoor toilets, only electricity has been brought to the hogan, which is not insulated but which boasts a refrigerator. The floor has been covered with loose linoleum tiles, and the portable toilet occupies space in the cooking area.

This home built of modern materials has neither windows nor insulation. It does, however, have electricity. The owner is a practicing ceremonialist despite the fact that both his wife and he suffer from crippling arthritis.

Some modern hogans can accommodate the beds and equipment of two invalids as well as comfortable tables and chairs without crowding.

Houses with drywall construction may have concealed electric wiring but may still not have running water or indoor toilets. Wheelchairs always take up space, although the sandy and rough terrain does not permit their use outside the dwelling. In fact, the contrast between the technologically sophisticated items provided the elderly and the harsh home environment is striking.

The environments provided by houses are not necessarily superior to those of the circular hogan. Although furniture fits more readily into a rectangular space, the houses are difficult to heat with wood-burning stoves, and walls and floors may be unfinished.

This home is equipped with electricity, running water, and an indoor toilet. It is light and airy, and it has a modern kitchen, good storage space, and enough room for a variety of activities, including weaving. Very few Navajos, however, are able to afford anything approaching what health providers consider adequate housing.

▸▸ 5 ◂◂

The Prevalence of
Diagnosed Hypertension

FOR MANY YEARS, high blood pressure has been thought to be caused, in part at least, by psychosocial stress. It is a significant risk factor for coronary heart disease and cerebrovascular disease, and in preindustrial rural populations in which these two diseases are not common, it has often been used as a measure of the impact of social change on health status (Marmot 1980). In general, it has been observed that among such people, those who are most exposed to social and cultural change are the most likely to become hypertensive. Cassel (1974:204–205) noted that "The reasons that among certain populations blood pressures are low, do not appear to rise with age, and change upon migration have so far escaped us." He went on to point out that there were, broadly speaking, two categories of explanation. The first has to do with the idea that "insulated" populations with low blood pressures and a constant prevalence of hypertension across age groups are characterized by diets low in salt, by adequate exercise, and by little or no obesity. The alternative explanation is that psychosocial factors are important in the etiology of hypertension. In insulated societies there is a "coherent value system which remains relatively unchallenged during the lifetime of the oldest inhabitants." Migration exposes an individual to a society with different values and adaptations learned early in life "can no longer be used to express normal behavioral urges, and this in turn creates repeated autonomic system arousal" (Cassel 1974).

It is with the second set of hypotheses that this chapter is concerned, especially with the hypothesis that links the low blood pressures found in many preindustrial societies to their "coherent value systems" and a subsequent rise in blood pressure to the disintegration of those systems when they are challenged by exposure to a dissimilar value system. Since, as we observe in chapter 1, such a change is often assumed to lead to the dismantling of the supportive extended family, we are concerned here with this issue as well.

Change brought about by sustained contact with another culture is generally referred to as acculturation, a term with a long and confused history in the social sciences. When originally used in Germany in 1910 by Walter Krickeberg to refer to the process of the development of a common basic culture among the tribes of diverse origin found on the upper Rio Xingu (Krickeberg, quoted in Buschan 1910:97–98), the term was free of any connotation of disintegration or psychosocial stress. The first systematic definition was that presented by Redfield, Linton, and Herskowitz (1936): "Acculturation comprehends those phenomena which result when groups of individuals having different cultures come into continuous first hand contact, with subsequent changes in the culture patterns of both groups" (quoted in Beals 1953:626). Despite considerable dissatisfaction with such a vague formulation, this is the definition most used today (see Oliver 1981:372–373, 389).

As used by most anthropologists, the process of acculturation applies to whole societies or parts of societies and does not imply that the final stage of the process must necessarily be assimilation. Equally possible is the development of entirely new cultural configurations. Nor does the concept imply the disintegration of the culture, although, because so many acculturation studies have dealt with the experiences of colonized peoples, this has often been the case.

Though formulated to describe changes undergone by whole cultures, it was almost inevitable that the term would be used to describe individuals. The more traits of the contact culture displayed by an individual, the more he was said to be acculturated. In effect, a semiquantified, one-dimensional index of acculturation has come into use which assigns a value of zero to the precontact condition assumed still to exist for some individuals and a maximum score to the state of total assimilation. Thus, "more" or "most acculturated" seems to refer to the individual who is the most like individuals in the other, usually dominant society.

The indicators of acculturation are almost always observable. That is, while inner states may be inferred, the indicators involve such attributes as clothing, level of education, religion, and involvement in the economic institutions of the contact society. Several assumptions are implied when the term is used in this manner: (1) As acculturation is often characterized by cultural disintegration, so must the degree of acculturation measure personal anomie and psychological stress. (2) Despite the fact that no observed individual has possessed both a precontact personality and a postcontact, acculturated one, those individuals who exhibit few or none of the traits chosen to measure acculturation are assumed to represent the "unstressed" precontact personality type. (3) Precontact societies are homogenous, and in consequence, the individuals in them are all so much alike that a description of the aboriginal culture can be used to make inferences about what "unacculturated" individuals are like at the time of observation, although this is most often some generations or even centuries after initial contact or conquest. (4) The precontact society, because it was "integrated," must also have been free of stress.

Without denying that these assumptions may be well founded in some instances, it is impossible to test their validity if a composite index of acculturation is employed. Each of the traits thought to be important to the processes of acculturation must be tested separately against the postulated dependent variable. Equally important is the fact that the individuals who comprise the study population occupy different statuses in their society. In the case of Navajos, for example, Aberle (1966) found that the wealthier among them suffered more from enforced livestock reduction in the 1930s than did the less wealthy and were, in consequence, more likely to join the nativistic peyotist religion than were the less wealthy. Similarly, Henderson (1985) found that the children of larger stock owners were more likely to become educated, get better jobs, and leave the reservation than were the children of the smaller stock owners.

Economic status was an important determinant of the acculturation experiences of the generation included in the present study, as well as of their parents and children. Our respondents were either just approaching or had already attained their maximum economic worth when the enforced stock reduction program was inaugurated in the late 1930s. The sudden destruction of their livelihood, which was thought necessary by government experts in order to save the range from overgrazing, deprived them of all means of support without providing viable alternatives. It is commonly regarded as perhaps the most traumatic event in Navajo history in this century. As neither schools nor employment opportunities were widely available, they could not easily become "acculturated." Yet they were certainly disoriented and stressed. Their children and grandchildren, on the other hand, reached maturity in a world that offered education and, to an extent, modern means of making a living. More of them know English and have more years of education and experience in the world of wage work and the cash economy. Which generation then suffered the most stress? The parents—so often called "traditional" and used to represent the unstressed, homogenous, prereservation society of the early nineteenth century if not the precontact society of the seventeenth century—had suffered a catastrophe in their own lives. The "acculturated" children tended to experience a disjunction between their own and their parents' values as they faced the contemporary world's challenges and opportunities.

A related hypothesis mentioned by Cassel—that migration to a "more developed society" with a value system different from the one in which the individual was originally socialized is causally related to the development of hypertension—implies that the society of origin is likely to have been one in which appropriate adaptations were learned early. But migration may also be viewed as an opportunity to escape from a repressive situation, and social change introduced into a society may have a similar effect.

For example, several of the studies cited in chapter 1 suggest that social change may not invariably have detrimental effects on health in general or blood pressure levels in particular (Beaglehole et al. 1977; Suzman et al. 1980; Joseph et al. 1983). More significant for our present purposes, they suggest that traditional societies are not necessarily homogenous and that social change may influence people differentially, depending on their place in their own society and the one to which they migrate. Patterns of blood pressure change among Navajos illustrate this point.

At least three field studies of blood pressure among Navajos have been published. The earliest, by Fulmer and Roberts (1963), was done at Many Farms between 1956 and 1962. It is often cited as one of those which show that in an isolated, preindustrial population, blood pressures are on average low and do not increase with age. A second, done on the eastern end of the reservation in 1977 (DeStefano et al. 1979), showed that mean pressures were elevated at all ages compared to those reported by Fulmer and Roberts roughly twenty years earlier. Most striking was the elevation of blood pressure among young adult men. Yet a third study, which followed migrants from the reservation to an urban area, showed that blood pressure did not differ among premigrants and nonmigrants on the reservation and that the blood pressure of migrants increased upon arrival in the city but that elevated pressure was not related to the length of time an individual had lived in the city (Alfred 1970). This study did not deal with diagnoses of hypertension but simply with group means. Thus, while blood pressure did increase a few mm Hg, no data are presented on the prevalence or incidence of hypertension.

While the study of migrants did show the expected increase in blood pressure, the field study on the eastern end of the reservation failed to show the expected relationships between blood pressure and some admittedly crude measures of acculturation. Indeed, among women systolic blood pressure decreased somewhat with increasing degrees of acculturation (DeStefano et al. 1979). There was also a slight but significant trend among women for blood pressure to increase with age. Weight, too, was positively associated with blood pressure, more so for men than women, and alcohol use was associated with elevated blood pressure among men. Alcohol use was ascertained simply by asking whether people did or did not drink, and the use of alcohol was assumed to be a measure of acculturation. We have shown elsewhere, however, that this is a very questionable assumption (Levy and Kunitz 1974). Heavy drinking is common among Navajo men regardless of their degree of acculturation (however measured) and is a pattern that has been observed in "traditional" Navajo settings for at least a century.

On the other hand, the high mean blood pressure among young adult men lends some support to the notion that this group is the most vulnerable to strains within Navajo society as well as to those emanating from the larger society. This same age group experiences the highest accident, suicide, and cirrhosis mortality rates and is the most highly involved in homicides. So far as we can determine, many of these are old patterns, and they suggest that young men in a matrilineal, matrilocal society may be especially marginal and therefore especially vulnerable to a variety of problems. If this is so, then migration to the larger society may be beneficial if there is access to jobs, enhanced security, and so on. Unhappily, this is often not the case.

Navajo women, however, have tended to have a more secure place in their traditional society than is likely to be accorded them in the larger Anglo-American society. The mother-daughter bond is especially significant; typically women remain in their families of origin upon marrying, with their husbands moving to join them. They have also typically owned their own livestock and retained rights of decision making regarding their property. Migration—even to a reservation or border town—may therefore remove them from sources of support and place them in a more vulnerable position than would have been the case had they remained at home. If this is so, then acculturation among women might place them at especially high risk. The data from the three studies among Navajos cited above are not entirely satisfactory in this regard since the samples were small to begin with and subdividing by age, sex, and degree of acculturation reduced the size even more, making inferences very uncertain.

Remember that our sample was drawn from all those people who were 65 years old and above in 1982, who lived in the Tuba City Service Unit, and who had had at least one outpatient visit in the preceding ten years. Conceivably, by choosing the sample in this way we did not include people who had never had any contact with the Public Health Service system of medical care, by far the most significant source of services on the reservation. This is unlikely to have led to significant bias, however, since it seems improbable that a substantial proportion of the population would not have had contact with a health care provider at least once in ten years.

Even among the people we did sample, possible sources of bias abound. Diagnoses of hypertension were gleaned from the medical records. We did not do a field survey of blood pressures. Thus there may be ascertainment bias: some individuals may have had more opportunity than others to be diagnosed simply by virtue of their patterns of health care utilization. We have been unable to discover any characteristics that consistently distinguish high users of services from those who use services infrequently. Moreover, if hypertensives were found to be high users of services, it is as likely that it would be the consequence of having been diagnosed hypertensive. In fact, hypertensives and normotensives do not differ with respect to hospital (1980–1983) and clinic (1958–1983) use, self-reported level of function (on the SIP scale), or mean and median distance they live from the hospital (all controlling for sex). Furthermore, May and Smith (1988:326) reviewed a number of studies on the Navajo Reservation and pointed out that "household surveys of health conditions among

Table 5.1. Prevalence of Diagnosed Hypertension by Age and Sex

Age	Men		Women	
	Hypertensive	Normotensive	Hypertensive	Normotensive
Below age 75	15 (75%)	56 (53%)	14 (54%)	69 (58%)
Age 75 to 84	5 (25%)	36 (35%)	8 (31%)	33 (27%)
Age 85 and above	0	13 (12%)	4 (15%)	18 (15%)

the Navajo in the late 1970s yielded data that were virtually identical to patient care data from IHS clinics." Thus there is some reason to believe that ascertainment bias, while potentially a problem, is not overwhelmingly significant.

In addition, there may be no rigorously applied standard for either taking blood pressure or defining hypertension in hospitals and clinics. With many people taking the measurements, there is no guarantee of uniformity. On the other hand, a diagnosis of hypertension can only be made and entered on the chart by a physician, though others may have initially screened the patient. This narrows considerably the number of people involved and increases the chance that methods and definitions will be less heterogenous than originally might have been thought. Moreover, a diagnosis of hypertension in the facility in which we worked is not made on the basis of only one casual measurement, which in fact is more likely to have been the case in the field studies. Several readings of a diastolic pressure of more than 90 mm Hg over a period of several months are necessary. Indeed, our method of case finding is likely to be more conservative than a field study. Thus, the prevalence of hypertension in the study population may be higher than we indicate below.

Table 5.1 displays the prevalence in our sample of diagnosed cases of hypertension by age and sex. There is no significant difference between men and women in proportion of diagnosed hypertensives (about 17 percent), nor is there a significant difference among age groups. The prevalence is substantially lower than in the general U.S. population of the same age, in which it is 31.5 percent among men and 43.4 percent among women (Verbrugge 1985:159).

It is useful to compare our results with those of previous studies, even knowing that methods and definitions may not be precisely the same. The criteria for hypertension used in the Many Farms study were those recommended by the Conference on Methodology in

Table 5.2. Prevalence of Hypertension in Three Studies

A. Individuals age 65 years and above, Many Farms, 1956–1962, and Tuba City, 1983	Hypertensive	Normotensive
Men		
Many Farms	5	20
Tuba City	25	105
$\chi^2 = 0.035$; df = 1; $p > .8$		
Women		
Many Farms	1	41
Tuba City	26	120
$\chi^2 = 5.11$; df = 1; $p < .025$		

B. Many Farms, 1956–1962 and eastern reservation, 1977	Hypertensive	Normotensive
Age 30–59		
Many Farms	11	326
Eastern reservation	76	292
$\chi^2 = 43.3$; df = 1; $p < .001$		
Age 60 and above		
Many Farms	10	93
Eastern reservation	9	63
$\chi^2 = 0.11$; df = 1; $p = .7$		

Epidemiological Studies of Cardiovascular Disease (Committee on Criteria 1960:23). Normotension was defined as a systolic pressure below 140 mm Hg and a diastolic below 90 mm Hg. Hypertension was defined as a systolic pressure over 160 mm Hg or a diastolic pressure of 95 mm Hg or above, or both. Borderline hypertension was defined as "systolic blood pressure . . . below 160 mm Hg and . . . diastolic blood pressure . . . below 95 mm Hg, but they are not simultaneously below both 140 mm Hg. systolic and 90 mm Hg. diastolic." It appears that in the calculations of the data they collected from the Many Farms population, Fulmer and Roberts (1963) considered borderline hypertension and hypertension as one category, thus making their definition of hypertension comparable to the one used in the present study.

We compared the earlier Many Farms samples with that from Tuba City and found that although there was no difference among men, there were significantly more hypertensive women in the more recent period than in the earlier (Table 5.2). In contrast, DeStefano et al. (1979) found that on the eastern end of the reservation in 1977 the prevalence of hypertension among men and women 60 years of age and above was the same as among men and women at Many Farms in 1956–1962. The difference between the people aged 30 to 59 was accounted for by men. There were no differences between the two groups of women.

These patterns are difficult to interpret. DeStefano et al. inferred that there had been a slight rise in blood pressure among men between 1956–1962 and 1977 but none among women. They pointed out, however, that the Many Farms study was of virtually all adults in one community, whereas theirs was done with volunteers at clinics, chapter meetings, rodeos, and other public places. Inasmuch as our data were gathered from a carefully selected sample from several communities, they are more nearly similar to the Many Farms data. On the other hand, since they are from hospital and clinic records in which diagnoses were made conservatively after several measurements, the method of case ascertainment is not comparable.

In general, when considering the figures from all three data sets for people in their sixties and above, the results are consistent in showing no differences among men. The results for women are inconsistent; one shows no increase while the other shows a significant increase. Nonetheless, given the differences in study design as well as regional differences among Navajo communities, it is wise not to assert too strenuously that a significant increase has occurred among older women.

We shall return to the issue of changing prevalence after we have described the associations in our sample between hypertension and a number of variables usually considered to be measures of acculturation: place and extent of education, English language ability, military service, residence off-reservation, involvement in wage work, use of alcohol, religious beliefs and practices, livestock ownership, and social isolation.

With respect to education, we have information on the number of years of schooling as well as whether people attended off-reservation boarding schools. The boarding school experience is said to have been

Table 5.3. Years of Education of Normotensives and Hypertensives

Years of Education	Men		Women	
	Normotensive	Hypertensive	Normotensive	Hypertensive
0	55 (53%)	11 (55%)	94 (79%)	16 (64%)
1 to 8	38 (37%)	6 (30%)	18 (15%)	4 (16%)
9 and above	10 (10%)	3 (15%)	7 (6%)	5 (20%)
	$\chi^2 = 0.674$		$\chi^2 = 5.559$	
	df = 2		df = 2	
	$p = .71$		$p = .06$	

Note: Unknowns excluded.

especially traumatic, intentionally removing people from their families and culture with an eye to making them over into Anglo-Americans. Similarly, the number of years of education is often thought to be a measure of the degree to which Navajo people have been influenced by alien values. For males, years of education was unrelated to hypertension (Table 5.3), but whether a woman had nine or more years of education (Table 5.3) or attended an off-reservation school (Table 5.4) does tend to be associated with hypertension.

Our interviewers and interpreters rated English language ability on a five-point scale from fluent in English to no English competency. Because these ratings were intuitive at best, we divided the men and women as close to the median as possible (Table 5.5). As with place of schooling, there was an effect on women but not men. Women with no English competency were significantly less likely to have been diagnosed hypertensive than were women with some English ability.

Military experience has often been said to be an important acculturating experience. Vogt (1951) showed that returning Navajo and Zuni World War II veterans had many problems reintegrating into their respective tribes, for example. We found no significant relationship between military service and hypertension, however.

Judging by the various studies of the relationship between migration and hypertension, we might reasonably expect that people with a history of off-reservation residence would be more likely to be hypertensive than people who have spent all their lives on the reservation. In addition, it is reasonable to expect that among those who have lived off-reservation, those who spent the longest time away would be

Table 5.4. Place of Education of Normotensives and Hypertensives

	Men		Women	
Attended Off-Reservation Boarding School	Normotensive	Hypertensive	Normotensive	Hypertensive
Yes	15 (15%)	4 (20%)	11 (9%)	6 (25%)
No	82 (85%)	16 (80%)	105 (91%)	18 (75%)
	$\chi^2 = 0.251$		$\chi^2 = 4.488$	
	$df = 1$		$df = 1$	
	$p = .61$		$p = .03$	

Note: Unknowns excluded.

most likely to be hypertensive. There was no relationship for women between having lived off-reservation at least a year and subsequently being diagnosed as hypertensive (Table 5.6). For men, the results were significant but not in the predicted direction. Those who spent a year or more off-reservation tended to have a lower prevalence of diagnosed hypertension than those who remained on the reservation.

When we considered only those who spent a year or more off-reservation and compared the hypertensives and normotensives with regard to the cumulative number of years away (by both the Mann-Whitney U-test and t-test), we found no significant differences for either sex. Nor could we find a difference between hypertensives and normotensives according to whether they ever had a wage job off-reservation.

Previously we noted that one study of Navajos reported that alcohol use was associated with hypertension in men but not in women. It is unfortunate that we did not ask as many questions about alcohol use as might, in retrospect, have been desirable. For a considerable number of women, we have no information regarding drinking patterns, and among the women from whom we do have information, very few were drinking at the time of interview. With the information at hand, however, we found that, while for men there was no relationship, there was quite a strong one for women (Table 5.7). Of the five women who were reported to be still using alcohol at the time of the study, four had been diagnosed as hypertensive. While this is only a small proportion of the hypertensive women in our sample, it represents a very significant proportion of those who use alcohol. These

Table 5.5. English Language Ability of Normotensives and Hypertensives

	Men		Women	
Language Ability	*Normotensive*	*Hypertensive*	*Normotensive*	*Hypertensive*
1 Fluent in English	12	6	7	4
2	14	3	7	2
3	29	1	13	2
4	39	8	23	9
5 No English	9	2	68	8
	$\chi^2 = 0.06$		$\chi^2 = 4.46$	
	df = 1		df = 1	
	p = .99		*p* = .04	

Note: Unknowns excluded.

data are congruent with observations we have reported elsewhere (Levy and Kunitz 1974) that Navajo women are much less likely than men to drink but that when they do drink, they are much more likely to do it for psychopathological reasons, and it is much more likely to cause them serious problems.

One of the most widely accepted measures of acculturation is the degree to which people adhere to their traditional religious beliefs. We might therefore expect that if acculturation is related to the prevalence of hypertension, the most traditional Navajos would have lower rates than anyone else. When we compared Christians, Traditionals, and people with mixed religious affiliations, however, we could find no significant differences whatever.

We also compared hypertensives and normotensives (controlling for sex) on the Religious Professional Participation Scale described in chapter 3. The expectation was that the most knowledgeable people would be the least likely to be hypertensive, but again no differences were found. Moreover, when male ceremonialists were compared with controls matched for age and sex, the proportion of hypertensives was found not to differ significantly between the two groups. Thus, by these measures Navajo traditionalism is not associated with a reduced level of hypertension.

Livestock ownership is one of the hallmarks of the Navajo tradition. Thus we might expect that people living in camps owning a lot of livestock would have a lower prevalence of hypertension than peo-

Table 5.6. Off-Reservation Residence for at Least One Year of Normotensives and Hypertensives

	Men		Women	
Off-Reservation Residence	Normotensive	Hypertensive	Normotensive	Hypertensive
Yes	75 (73%)	10 (50%)	20 (17%)	7 (27%)
No	28 (27%)	10 (50%)	98 (83%)	19 (73%)
	$\chi^2 = 4.08$		$\chi^2 = 1.391$	
	df = 1		df = 1	
	p = .04		p = .238	

Note: Unknowns excluded.

ple living in camps owning little or no livestock, but this expectation is not supported by the data. Similarly, when cattle rather than sheep ownership was considered, the differences were again not significant. It is questionable, of course, whether current livestock holding is a measure of acculturation. The pastoral economy is no longer economically viable, and differences in sheep holdings are small. It would be preferable to know the herd size of the respondent or his or her parents prior to stock reduction if only to determine status prior to forced change. Currently, large herds are most often made possible by successful adaptation to wage work and the investment of income in cattle.

We have already noted that the process of acculturation is usually thought to involve a decline in support from the extended family. As a first step, therefore, we did a simple comparison of hypertensives and normotensives by camp size (by Mann-Whitney U-test, controlling for sex). There was no difference among men but a significant difference among women ($p = .042$), with normotensives living in larger camps than hypertensives. Similar results were obtained when the social isolation-integration index was used (Table 5.8). Among the most isolated women there was a significantly higher proportion of hypertensives than there was among the less isolated women. No differences were observed among the men.

Thus far we have examined the relationship between independent variables and hypertension one at a time, but there is some reason to expect that there may be joint effects. For example, we have shown that the most isolated women and the women who are best educated

Table 5.7. Alcohol Use Among Normotensives and Hypertensives

	Men		Women	
Alcohol Use	Normotensive	Hypertensive	Normotensive	Hypertensive
Unknown	35	6	17	1
Not currently drinking	51	9	101	21
Currently drinking	18	5	1	4
	$\chi^2 = 0.16$		$\chi^2 = 8.33$	
	df = 1		df = 1	
	$p = .70$		$p = .009$	

have a higher prevalence of hypertension than other women. We might expect that women who are both relatively well educated and most isolated would be at particular risk (Table 5.9). First, forgetting about hypertension for a moment, there was no difference among either men or women in the relationship between education and isolation or integration. People with nine years or more of education were as likely to have much contact with kin as those with less education. Second, the number of people in the highest risk group (most isolated and best educated) was very small. Third, the interactions between isolation or integration and education were as expected for women, but no relationship was observed among men, which is to say that for women the effects of low education and low social isolation are multiplicative and reduce the risk of hypertension (by 16-fold) more than either alone. Small numbers caution against exuberance in interpreting the results, however.

A number of sources of potential bias have already been called to attention. Case ascertainment is based on diagnoses made in hospitals and clinics. Conceivably, consistent biases in the utilization of health care could increase the likelihood that some people have a better chance than others of being observed frequently and therefore being diagnosed more accurately. We do not think this is the case, however, based on the comparisons we have been able to make. Moreover, the fact that the prevalence of hypertension in our sample is so similar to that observed in an independently conducted field study elsewhere on the reservation suggests that very few if any hypertensives have escaped detection.

We have said it is wise to be circumspect about asserting that there

Table 5.8. Hypertension by Social Isolation-Integration

	Men		Women	
Isolation-Integration	*Hypertensive*	*Normotensive*	*Hypertensive*	*Normotensive*
Low	3 (15%)	9 (9%)	8 (32%)	11 (10%)
Medium	9 (45%)	37 (37%)	13 (52%)	77 (68%)
High	8 (40%)	53 (53%)	4 (16%)	25 (22%)
	$\chi^2 = 1.29$		$\chi^2 = 8.55$	
	df = 2		df = 2	
	$p = .50$		$p = .015$	

Note: Unknowns excluded.

has been an increase in the prevalence of hypertension among women. Not only differences in case ascertainment but also differences among populations across the reservation could explain the seeming increase. A study in Tuba City in 1956–62 might have revealed the same differences from the Many Farms population as we see now. Certainly as far back as the 1930s the populations differed markedly. People in District 10, where Many Farms is located, were more densely settled and more dependent on agriculture than people in Districts 1 and 3, who had larger flocks and herds and who were more dependent on livestock (Kunitz 1977a). Thus the trauma of stock reduction would presumably have had a more severe impact in Districts 1 and 3 than on 10, and different pressures may have been brought to bear on family organization and on the incentives to become involved in wage work and to obtain an education by people of the same generation in different areas of the reservation. With smaller flocks to begin with, the people aged 65 and above at Many Farms would conceivably have been less traumatized as young people in the 1930s than people of the same age whose families were more dependent on livestock. This is to say that if stock reduction forced people to alter their expectations radically and if such change is indeed stressful, one could at least make a plausible case that people in Districts 1 and 3 were more stressed than those in District 10. Further, if stress is an important factor in the etiology of hypertension, then hypertension may have been more prevalent in those districts as well. The current pattern among women, then, may not represent anything especially new.

These examples are meant to be illustrative, not explanatory. They

Table 5.9. Logistic Regression of Education, Social Isolation-Integration, and Hypertension

A. MEN

Isolation-Integration Score	Education			
	0 to 8 Years		9 Years	
	Hypertensive	*Normotensive*	*Hypertensive*	*Normotensive*
1	3	8	0	1
2–3	14	82	3	8

Predictor Variable	Estimate in Logistic Scale	Standard Error	Estimate in Odds Scale	95% Confidence Interval
Mean	–1.543	0.6606		
Education	0.3732	0.7061	1.45	(0.35, 5.96)
Isolation-Integration	0.1665	0.6972	1.18	(0.29, 4.76)

B. WOMEN

Isolation-Integration Score	Education			
	0 to 8 Years		9 Years	
	Hypertensive	*Normotensive*	*Hypertensive*	*Normotensive*
1	6	12	1	1
2–3	13	98	4	7

Predictor Variable	Estimate in Logistic Scale	Standard Error	Estimate in Odds Scale	95% Confidence Interval
Mean	–0.7627	0.4832		
Education	1.327	0.6387	3.77	(1.05, 13.52)
Isolation-Integration	–1.234	0.5490	3.43	(1.14, 10.30)

Note: Unknowns excluded.

are speculative and are offered only to emphasize that the Navajo population is heterogenous. Thus comparisons across both time and space must be viewed critically and thus our reluctance to assert unequivocally that a true increase in prevalence has occurred.

Turning now to a consideration of the pattern of hypertension in our sample, we are faced with the question of why there is a consistent association with measures of acculturation and social isolation among women but not among men. We have suggested that Navajo men may be more vulnerable than women to stressful events within their own society because of their somewhat more marginal position within the traditional family organization. For them, wage work could conceivably represent an opportunity, though discrimination and lack of preparation too often militate against such a happy outcome. For women, involvement in the educational system and wage work may represent the loss of a secure place and thus may make them more vulnerable to hypertension. To deal with that possibility, one must know something of the circumstances leading women of this generation to have gone to school and for varying lengths of time.

In the region in which we worked, particularly in District 1, there is evidence that wealthy stock owners encouraged both sons and daughters to obtain an education so that they could deal more effectively with Anglos (Henderson 1985). This was true even before stock reduction, and it continued to be true afterward. Therefore one might expect the hypertensive women to have come from wealthier families than normotensive women. Unfortunately, our data on prereduction livestock holdings are incomplete. The data we do have, however, show no relationship between this variable and hypertension.

We have suggested that acculturation may have different consequences for men and women. It is possible, however, that acculturation is important for men as well but that selective mortality at younger ages has obscured the effect in our elderly sample. This is a prevalence study. Recall that in the field study by DeStefano et al. (1979), men below age 60 had a 24 percent prevalence of hypertension and that age-specific mortality rates of Navajo men are higher than those of women throughout most of adulthood (Kunitz 1983). Hypertensive men may die earlier than normotensive men, resulting in a reduction in the proportion of hypertensive men at old age. If the men who die are disproportionately hypertensive and are also disproportionately acculturated, then the failure to show a difference among men in our sample may simply be the result of earlier selection.

If this were the case, we would expect that (1) young adult hypertensive men surveyed by DeStefano et al. would have been more acculturated than normotensive men, and (2) as a result of continuing selective mortality there would have been a difference in the proportions of hypertensive men above and below the age of 75 in our sample, with significantly fewer being found in the older group. We do not observe either of these to be true. We believe that if the difference in prevalence between men above and below age 60 (24 vs. 17 percent) is in fact real (it is not statistically significant), it is more likely the result of increasing rates in successive cohorts than selective mortality among young adult men. Thus we do not think differential mortality of acculturated, prehypertensive or hypertensive men at young ages explains our results.

We noted at the outset that there are two competing hypotheses regarding the etiology of hypertension in transitional societies. The first has to do with dietary and other behavioral changes, the second with psychosocial stress. Our data do not permit an examination of the first. It is entirely possible that acculturated women are more obese and less physically active than other women and that this enhances their chance of developing hypertension. Though we cannot reject the possibility, it is unlikely that this alone can explain our results, because the association between being overweight and being hypertensive, while significant, seems to be weak among the Navajo women examined by DeStefano et al. Moreover, there is no reason why an association between being overweight and being acculturated should be limited to women. If there is an association, it should exist among men also, among whom there seems to be a much stronger association between being overweight and being hypertensive. Thus, if the explanation were true for women, it should be equally true for men. That there is no association between hypertension and measures of acculturation among men suggests (but does not prove) that obesity is at least not the only intermediate link in the chain.

These results suggest that Cassel's alternative explanations of hypertension in previously insulated populations may not cover the full range of possibilities. They fail to include a consideration of the significance of either internal differentiation of tribal societies or the opportunities as well as the costs of social change. The women in our sample seem to confirm the notion that change is associated with an increased risk of hypertension. The data for the men are less clear but provide some evidence that wage work may have provided a way out of potentially stressful situations for some.

Our results also support the notion we have suggested previously that we are observing several different forms of morbidity. Some, like physical functioning as measured by high SIP scores, may be part of the usual aging process. Others that may or may not be reflected in high scores are considered specific nosographic entities: respiratory and renal failure, hypertension, and depression. Only a few of these morbid processes appear to be associated with psychosocial variables, and even at that it is not certain that the association is causal. A major problem, of course, is that so far we have been describing a prevalence study. In the next chapter, therefore, we turn our attention to mortality in the several years after interview in order to assess more closely its causal relationship, if any, with psychosocial factors, most notably social isolation and integration.

In sum, then, it is clear that social isolation and acculturation as measured by level of education and skill in English put women but not men at risk for hypertension. Men who have lived off-reservation, in fact, are less at risk for hypertension than are men who have not had this acculturational experience. Despite the need for caution in interpreting these results, the most likely explanation is that Navajo men are exposed to as much stress in the more "traditional" matrilineal society as in the more acculturated world of wage work and off-reservation living. It might even be argued that for many men, living in neolocal families and having gained experience in the Anglo world lessens the tensions generated by life among the kinsmen of their wives. The converse also fits the data: that women were more secure in the traditional matrilocal extended family and were exposed to more stress when forced to leave this protective environment.

►► 6 ◄◄

MORTALITY

TWO ISSUES CONCERN US in this chapter. One is related to the central problem with which we began: the relationship between social support and health. The follow-up study of mortality allows us to use the measures of involvement with others as predictors of the incidence of death, which is clearly preferable to prevalence data. The other has to do with the puzzling questions raised in chapter 3: whether Navajos have lower mortality rates at older ages than non-Indians, and if they do, whether elderly Navajos are in better or worse health than non-Indians as a result. We begin with a description of causes and rates of death in the entire tribal population 65 and above both to determine whether a mortality "crossover" exists among Navajos and to assess how similar our sample is to the entire population.

The size and remoteness of the Navajo Reservation have made the population notoriously difficult to enumerate, and language barriers and a lack of adequate records have made the reporting of age at least as difficult. Both problems have been a source of frustration for researchers and bureaucrats alike for decades. Considering the difficulties, it is remarkable that there has been a good deal of consistency in estimates of the proportion of the Navajo population 65 years of age and above over the past 70 to 80 years. Despite undoubted inaccuracies, it is noteworthy that all estimates place the proportion 65 and above at between 3.0 and 4.5 percent. In contrast, the proportion 65 and above in the entire U.S. population was 11.3 percent in 1980. Thus, although the population has grown at a rapid rate during the course of this century, there is no evidence that the age structure has changed dramatically.[1]

The Navajos are still a young population, and fertility seems to have been high until the post–World War II years, at which time it began a slow decline from more than 40 per 1,000 to considerably less than 30 per 1,000 at present. During the same period, however, infant mortality began a very steep decline from about 140 to 17 per 1,000 live births. Declining infant and child mortality offset declining fertility so that the overall impact was of continuing rapid population growth and a broad-based age pyramid. In the future, as fertility continues to fall more rapidly than mortality, the age structure will gradually be transformed into one more nearly resembling that of the general U.S. population (Broudy and May 1983). Of course, the number of people 65 and above has increased, though estimates of the size of this age group vary widely even for the period from 1972 through 1980. Nonetheless, it is safe to assert that changes in the perceived or actual conditions of the elderly are unlikely to be due to a major change in age structure over the past 70 years.

Not only has infant mortality declined but so has the mortality rate for the entire population, from perhaps 10–11 per 1,000 in 1945 to 6–7 per 1,000 by the early 1980s (Kunitz 1983). There is no evidence, however, that mortality among those 65 and above has changed very dramatically, though it must be emphasized that the data are not entirely adequate. The U.S. Public Health Service (1957) estimated that average annual age-specific mortality of Navajos 65 and above was 30.6 per 1,000 in the population on the Arizona portion of the reservation in 1949–53 (including a very small proportion of Hopis), 37.6 in the New Mexico Navajo population, and 50 in the Utah Navajo population. We have estimated the average annual age-specific rate in 1972–78 to lie between 34 and 48 per 1,000 people 65 and above.[2] Considering the difficulty of data collection and enumeration, the differences are not very impressive.

Using the number of people in each age group based on the proportions estimated by Carr (1978), we applied age-specific death rates for the entire U.S. population to the two estimates of the Navajo population in five-year segments starting at age 65 (Table 6.1). Even using the extremely low population estimate of 4,000, the observed number of deaths is not significantly different from that expected in any age group.

Table 6.1. Observed and Expected Deaths of Navajos Age 65 and Above, 1972–1978

Age	Number of Navajo Deaths 1972–1978	Average per Year	1976 U.S. Death Rate per 1,000[a]	Low Population Estimate[b]	Expected Deaths per Year Based on Low Population Estimate	High Population Estimate[c]	Expected Deaths per Year Based on High Population Estimate
65–69	291	42	25.4	1,775	45	2,664	68
70–74	269	38	39.5	945	37	1,416	56
75–79	260	37	61.9	588	36	882	55
80–84	210	30	90.3	342	31	516	47
85 and above	420	60	154.9	348	54	522	81

Source: U.S. Public Health Service 1978.
[b]Population estimate of 4,000 Navajos age 65 and above in 1975.
[c]Population estimate of 6,000 Navajos age 65 and above in 1975.

Though the population data are far from adequate and the mortality data may be underreported to an unknown but not extravagant degree, the evidence is reasonably good that mortality rates among elderly Navajos are no higher than the rates among non-Indians of the same age and are almost certainly lower. Since mortality at younger ages is higher among Navajos than among non-Navajos (Kunitz 1983), this is an instance of the mortality "crossover" that has been observed among black Americans as well as the subjects in cross-national studies (Wing et al. 1985; Weatherby et al. 1983), though the crossover seems to occur at younger ages among Navajos than it does among other populations.

Mortality crossover refers to the observation that among certain populations age-specific mortality is high at young and adult ages and relatively low at old age compared to mortality rates in some standard, usually relatively affluent, population. It is generally explained in the following way: If one assumes that biological life span does not differ significantly among races or cross-nationally, then mortality must rise at some age among populations in which it has been low through most of life. Generally it is relatively poor populations that experience high mortality in the young and adult years, presumably because of their exposure to a harsh environment, inadequate nutrition, and a lack of access to medical care.

Causes of death among populations experiencing the mortality crossover differ from those observed in more affluent populations. The former tend to die from so-called exogenous causes (e.g., infectious diseases and accidents), the latter from what are called endogenous causes (e.g., cardiovascular diseases and cancers). These terms are not ideal since they assume a causal explanation that, in the case of the so-called endogenous causes, is yet to be demonstrated.

These patterns are observed among the Navajo. Carr and Lee (1978) estimated that the elimination of motor vehicle accidents would increase Navajo male life expectancy at birth 5.17 years, and the elimination of all other accidents would add another 3.13 years. In contrast, the elimination of automobile accidents would have added only 0.93 year at birth to the life of white U.S. males in 1969–71. Conversely, the elimination of cardiovascular disease would have added 10.46 years of life at birth for white males and only 3.31 for Navajo males. Women manifest similar patterns, though they lose fewer years of life as a result of accidents than do men.

Similar contrasts with the non-Navajo population emerge when

Table 6.2. Leading Causes of Mortality of Navajos Age 65 and Above: Average Annual Rates per 100,000 Population, 1972–1978, Based on Low and High Population Estimates

Cause	Navajo			U.S. Population, 1976
	Number	*Low Rate[a]*	*High Rate[b]*	
Heart disease	242	576	864	2,393
Malignant neoplasms	174	414	621	979
Cerebrovascular disease	112	266	400	694
Accidents	150	357	535	104
Diabetes	33	78	117	108
Cirrhosis	12	28	43	36
Influenza/pneumonia	156	371	557	211
Arteriosclerosis	3	7	11	122
Total for all causes	1,450	3,452	5,178	5,429

[a]Based on 1975 population estimate of 6,000.
[b]Based on 1975 population estimate of 4,000.

we consider causes of death among the elderly (Table 6.2). Rates of heart disease, malignant neoplasms, and cerebrovascular diseases are all much higher among non-Navajos than even the highest estimated Navajo rates.

A combination of forces has worked a change in the sex ratio of the reservation population from the 1940s to the present: declining maternal mortality, increasing male mortality from accidents, and differential rates of emigration seem to have resulted in a shift such that women now outnumber men (Kunitz and Slocumb 1976). Although it is generally agreed that women outnumber men in the total population, there is disagreement as to whether the change has yet affected the oldest cohorts. Most figures suggest that men still predominate at ages above 65. The difference is not enormous, however, being on the order of 1 to 2 percent. If, for the sake of simplicity, we say that the numbers of men and women 65 and above are essentially equal, the average annual age-specific mortality rate for the period 1972–78 was between 38 and 54 per 1,000 for males and between 30 and 43 per 1,000 for females. There is, then, some evidence that male and female mor-

Table 6.3. Mortality by Age and Sex

	Age at Time of Follow-up			
	Below Age 75		*Age 75 and Above*	
Status at Time of Follow-up	*Men*	*Women*	*Men*	*Women*
Dead	8	0	14	15
Alive	40	56	62	75
	$\chi^2 = 10.111$		$\chi^2 = 0.0888$	
	df = 1		df = 1	
	$p < .01$		$p > .7$	

tality continue to differ in older age groups. Projections of the growth of the elderly population based on the assumption that current mortality trends will continue indicate that the proportion of men and women 65 and above will have shifted from approximate equality to 43 percent men and 57 percent women by the year 2,000 (Carr 1978).

The Mortality Experience of the Elderly

Our sample of respondents was interviewed during the twelve-month period September 1, 1982, to August 30, 1983. During that year and for the next three years, we followed their mortality experience. We used key informants, regular reviews of hospital records, and two reviews of death certificates in the State Health Department in Phoenix to ascertain death. The first death certificate review was done in April 1985 and the second in August 1986. The last wave of interviews of key informants was in June 1986. We have no reason to believe that any deaths went undiscovered during that period. All people were considered to have been under observation from the time of interview to the time of death or until June 30, 1986. The average number of months of observation was 37 per person.

By June 30, 1986, significantly more men than women below the age of 75 had died (Table 6.3). This is consistent with previous findings that women in this age group reported lower scores than men on the Sickness Impact Profile (SIP), as well as lower rates of hospital use.

Table 6.4. Observed and Expected Navajo Deaths by Age and Sex

Age	U.S. Population, Death Rate per 1,000 in 1976		Number of Navajos in 1982	Expected Deaths in 3 Years	Observed in 3 Years (Age at Time of Interview)
Men					
65–69	35.9	⎫ 45.1	71	9–10	10
70–74	54.3	⎭			
75–79	82.6	⎫			
80–84	115.2	⎬ 125.8	53	20	12
85 and above	179.8	⎭			
Women					
65–69	17.1	⎫ 22.8	83	6	2
70–74	28.6	⎭			
75–79	17.1	⎫			
80–84	76.3	⎬ 89.3	64	17	13
85 and above	143.1	⎭			

There was no significant difference between the sexes at ages 75 and above.

Thirty-seven people died during the period of observation, yielding an average annual rate of about 45 per 1,000, which is close to the top of the range we estimated for the entire Navajo population 65 years of age and above. When we applied the age-specific death rates for the entire U.S. population to the same five-year age intervals of the people in our sample, we noted that the total expected number of deaths (about 50) was higher than the observed number (37) and that the same was true in each age group (Table 6.4).

The people who died had significantly higher scores on all the SIP scales than those who were still alive. They had also been hospitalized more often, had spent more days in hospital, and had had more diagnostic tests. They did not score higher on the Depression scale, however. There was no difference between the two groups with respect to per capita or camp income, income from various sources, number of people per room, availability of conveniences such as running water and electricity, distance of residence from the nearest hospital, cattle and sheep holdings, or years of education.

Table 6.5. Mortality by Marital Status and Age

	Below Age 75		Age 75 and Above	
	Married	Unmarried	Married	Unmarried
Men				
Dead	6	2	7	7
Alive	3	9	52	10
	Fisher's exact test: $p < .05$		$\chi^2 = 7.545$ $(p < .01)$	
Women				
Dead	0	0	3	12
Alive	23	33	20	55
χ^2	—		0.292	
df	—		1	
p	—		> 0.5	

Unmarried men died at a significantly higher rate than did married men if they were 75 or above (Table 6.5). On the other hand, men under age 75 were more likely to die if they were married, although the finding was equivocal.[3] There were no differences between married and unmarried women regardless of age. Nor were there comparable differences when the number of children living in the camp, the number of households in the camp, generational depth of the camp, camp composition (neolocal or extended), and index of social isolation-integration were considered.

To explore the association between marriage and mortality further, we did several analyses. Kaplan-Meier survival curves for males by marital status and PHYSIP score show differences between married and unmarried men that are statistically significant ($p = .016$), using a one-tailed test because of the expectation that unmarried people are at greater risk of death than married people (Figure 6.1). For approximate tests of hypotheses, we used Cox proportional hazards regression. Under the regression model, single males encounter approximately 2.5 times the hazards of married males. This is reduced to 2.3 times greater after adjustment for a SIP score with 90 percent confidence limits (1.1, 4.8), and to 2.1 times greater after adjustment for both age and a SIP score with 90 percent confidence limits (1.0, 4.4).[4]

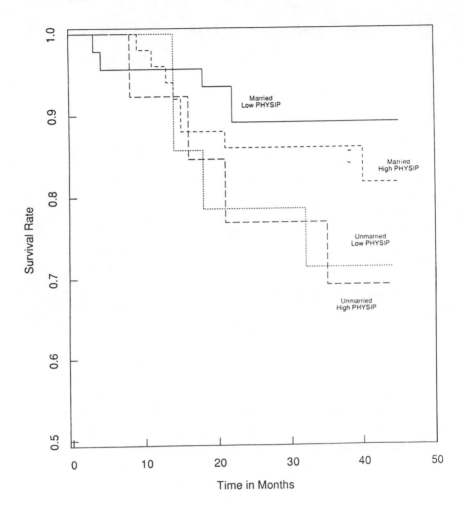

Figure 6.1. Survival Curves for Males by Marital Status and PHYSIP Score

The result of the Cox regression with age as one of the variables is equivocal, the lower limit of the confidence interval being 1.0. This reflects the fact that marital status and mortality seem to have a different relationship depending on age, a subject we return to below.

Comparable survival curves for women show that unmarried women with high SIP scores differ from the other three groups (Figure 6.2). Women in this group have an eight times greater hazard of

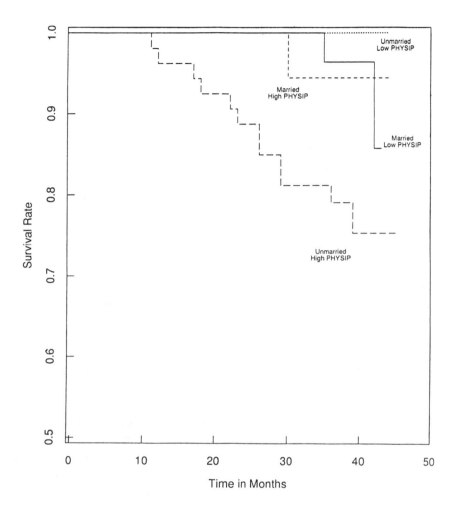

**Figure 6.2. Survival Curves for Females by Marital Status and PHYSIP
Score**

dying than the other three groups combined. We attempted an approximate age adjustment, and the relative hazards for those 75 and
above were approximately six times that of women below the age of
75, but even with an age variable in the model, the effect of the SIP
score remained strong. The effect of marital status essentially disap-
pears after adjustment for age. This result for women seems to be a

consequence of the fact that the younger women had the lowest SIP scores, experienced no deaths, and were also most likely to be married.

We must now ask why marital status is the only psychosocial variable significantly associated with an increased risk of death and why only among men 75 and above. One possibility is that the low mortality of elderly Navajos is the result of selection at younger ages such that only the healthiest survive. And if the survivors are particularly healthy, perhaps social interaction is simply irrelevant to enhanced survival. If this is the case, it must be sex-related, since marital status is associated with survival among men but not women.

There seem to be two somewhat different processes at work. With respect to mortality among men, several observations are noteworthy. The only people in our sample who died below age 75 were men. Men are more likely than women to be married at ages above and below 75. When SIP scores of deceased men and age-matched controls are compared, the men below 75 who died had significantly higher scores, but there was no difference between cases and controls 75 years of age and above. When number of hospital days is compared, the men under 75 who died had spent significantly more days in hospital than had the controls, whereas among older men there was again no difference. Thus there is evidence that among the younger men who died, some had serious disabling illnesses requiring lengthy hospital stays. Indeed, their physical disabilities were sufficiently great that being married was not protective. Older men who died did not differ from matched controls who did not die on these measures of severity of preexisting disease. This would seem to support the possibility that among men there is a selection process at work such that those below 75 who die are in discernibly worse health than those who do not die, whereas no such distinction can be made among the older men.

The situation is very different for the women. No women died below age 75, and this group had the lowest SIP scores and the lowest proportion that had been hospitalized. Among women 75 and above, very few were married. When women who died are compared with controls matched for age and sex, the former have significantly higher SIP scores but not significantly more days in hospital.

It appears, then, that one reason marital status makes a difference among men is that mortality is high enough and marital status sufficiently varied that its effect is discernible. Marital status may have a discernible "protective" effect only among men 75 and above because the men who died below that age were sufficiently sick that psycho-social factors were relatively less important. Among women, just the opposite pertains: In the age group in which death is common, marital status does not vary. Clearly, the two situations are related, for it is high mortality among younger men that results in the high frequency of unmarried women at older ages. This does not explain why mortality is higher among men than women; it simply contributes to part of an explanation of why no effect of marriage is observed among women.

Excess male mortality is not unique to the Navajos (Verbrugge 1985). In the course of the epidemiologic transition from high to low mortality regimes, female mortality generally declines more rapidly and to lower levels than does male mortality (Omran 1971). In low-mortality regimes such as exist in developed and some developing nations, female life expectancy is greater than male, and females outnumber males at all ages. There is no universally agreed upon explanation for the phenomenon, but it is usually attributed to differences in behavioral patterns, as suggested by the changing incidence of smoking and lung cancer among men and women in the United States, and deaths from accidents among Navajos (Kunitz 1983). How much of the difference is simply a matter of behavioral patterns such as these and how much is associated with biological differences between the sexes is by no means clear, however.

With respect to the protective effect of marriage among older men but not women, many observers have commented that among Navajos the preferred residence pattern has traditionally been matrilocal. Thus a multihousehold camp would ideally include a senior couple, their married daughters and their husbands and children, plus the senior couple's unmarried children. There may be a tendency for men who marry into such a unit to be peripheral to it and also to live at some remove from their own natal households.

While this pattern may have been preferred, it has never been universal. It is true, however, that the mother-daughter bond is an extremely important one, as our discussion of depression suggests, and it is worth considering whether unmarried men and women differ from married men and women in the degree to which they have contact with other kin. We would expect unmarried men to be the most isolated and unmarried women to be at least as closely connected with kin as married men and women, if not more so.

Unmarried men were significantly more likely than others to live in camps without their children (Table 6.6). On the other hand, unmar-

Table 6.6. Marital Status, Sex, and Number of Co-resident Children

No. of Children	Married Men	Married Women	Unmarried Men	Unmarried Women	Total
0	34	16	14	22	86
1	20	14	7	47	88
2 or more	42	15	6	30	93
Total	96	45	27	99	267

$\chi^2 = 21.863$

$df = 6$

$p < .01$

ried women were more likely than others to live with their children. Unmarried women were also more likely to live in multigenerational camps (data not shown). Of the 27 unmarried men, 6 lived in single-person camps. Of 99 unmarried women, 4 lived in single-person camps ($p < .01$). Thus men are more likely than women to be married, but when men are not married, they are more likely than unmarried women to live in isolation, not only from their children but from other people as well.

Only among men living with no children or only one child is being unmarried associated with a significantly increased risk of death (Table 6.7).[5] Among men living with two or more children, as well as among married and unmarried women regardless of the number of children with whom they live, there is no association between marital status and risk of death.

It is puzzling that being unmarried should be associated with an increased risk of death only among men living with no children or one child but not among women in the same situation. There is no evidence from the scaled instruments that we used to measure depression and level of functioning that there was a difference between married and unmarried men and women that would suggest that less healthy people were unmarried and thus at greater risk of dying. On the other hand, it was observed in the course of interviewing that men often denied depressive symptoms or used alcohol to mask them. This was not found to be the case among women. In reviewing our field notes and interviews in search of a possible explanation, we looked

Table 6.7. Mortality by Marital Status, Sex, and Number of Co-resident Children

Marital Status	No. Co-resident Children			
	0 or 1 Child		2 or More Children	
	Dead	Alive	Dead	Alive
Men				
Married	6	48	7	35
Unmarried	7	14	1	5
	$\chi^2 = 6.8^a$		$\chi^2 - 0.0^b$	
Women				
Married	2	28	1	14
Unmarried	9	60	3	27
	$\chi^2 = 1.62^b$		$\chi^2 = 0.08^b$	

Note: Unknowns excluded.
[a] $p < .05$
[b] Not significant

particularly for any mention of alcohol abuse. And indeed, of the 9 unmarried men who died, 5 had recent histories of excessive use. Of the 13 married men who died, only 1 was noted to have a recent history of alcohol abuse. Unfortunately, because alcohol use was not a central focus of the research to begin with, equally detailed histories were not taken from all respondents. Furthermore, this is a result discovered after the fact rather than a hypothesis with which we began. For both reasons, therefore, formal tests of significance would be inappropriate. We believe the finding to be a real one, however.

We have suggested elsewhere that heavy drinking among Navajo men generally ceases by the time they reach their late thirties or early forties (Levy and Kunitz 1974). Not all men stop or reduce their consumption, however, and some resume drinking as a consequence of a traumatic event, such as the death of a wife or a favorite son, both of which happened to men in our sample. Whatever the sequence— whether heavy drinking among elderly men maintains, exacerbates, or causes isolation—it seems likely that it contributes to both physical deterioration and increased risk of death.

THE MORTALITY CROSSOVER

We have shown that mortality among elderly Navajos is lower than among non-Indians of the same age. This raises several questions. First, do either or both sexes account for the effect? Second, what causes of death characterize this low-mortality population? Third, does high mortality at younger ages result in an especially healthy older population?

With respect to the first question, the evidence suggests that the crossover begins later for men than for women. The men with histories of recent excessive alcohol use did not die at younger ages than the men without such histories and thus do not seem to contribute to the delayed crossover effect in comparison with women.

As mortality rates decline and chronic, noninfectious diseases become more significant than infectious diseases, it becomes increasingly difficult to determine a single cause of death. Generally, multiple contributing causes are involved, particularly among elderly people. The problem is exacerbated in our sample because no autopsies were done and 11 people (30 percent) died at home without significant investigation of the circumstances. Causes of death were extracted from medical records and death certificates, although it is not clear how accurate many of these diagnoses were (Table 6.8). The cases diagnosed as heart failure (3), tuberculosis (1), natural causes (2), and cardiac arrest (1) all died at home and were investigated by a police coroner. Only one of them, a 91-year-old woman, had been in hospital during the study period, and she had been diagnosed then as having ischemic heart disease. The 66-year-old man who died of a presumed cardiac arrest had a history of chronic alcohol abuse and had a chronic subdural hematoma and cerebral atrophy. He was found dead in the shower. One of the men with heart failure was 65 at the time of interview, was in remarkably good health, and died while herding sheep. The 82-year-old woman diagnosed as having died from tuberculosis was found dead in bed, and her hospital record contained no evidence of active disease.

On the other hand, of the five cases of acute myocardial infarction, two were diagnosed in hospital and two died in cars while being transported to hospital and had histories compatible with myocardial infarction. The fifth died in a nursing home of aspiration pneumonia while in coma after an infarction. This person also had a history of ischemic heart disease and bouts of respiratory failure secondary to

Table 6.8. Causes of Death, 1983–1986

Cause	No. of Deaths
Heart Disease	
Acute myocardial infarction	5
"Heart failure"	3
Cardiorespiratory arrest	1
Cardiac arrest	1
Cerebrovascular accident	2
Respiratory	
Tuberculosis	1
Chronic obstructive pulmonary disease	2
Pneumonia	3
Genitourinary	
Renal Failure	3
Cancer	
Malignant mesothelioma	1
Accident	
Pedestrian struck by motor vehicle	3
Fall followed by subdural hematoma	1
Violence, exacerbating "debility"	1
Fall followed by fractured femur	1
Miscellaneous	
Unknown	5
"Natural causes"	2
Bubonic plague	1
Chronic comatose state and aspiration pneumonia	1

old tuberculosis. Likewise, the two cases attributed to respiratory failure had well-documented histories (one died in a nursing home, the other at home), as did the two cases who died of strokes (one in hospital, the other in a nursing home). Of the three cases of renal failure, two were clearly diabetic in origin, while the third was of unknown etiology. This person had pneumonia as the immediate cause of death.

Table 6.9. Causes of Death of Navajos Age 65 and Above, Many Farms, 1957–1961

Cause	Number of Deaths
Unknown	1
Pneumonia	6
Tubular necrosis, uremia	1
Metastatic cancer	1
Myocardial infarction	1
Diabetes-pyelonephritis	1
Accidental	1
Heart disease of unknown etiology	1

The man who was debilitated and had been badly beaten, probably by his alcoholic son, died in a nursing home. It is not certain that the beating contributed to his death, however, and it is with some reservation that we have listed it as due to violence. The 75-year-old man who died after a fall and a fractured femur had been in hospital for treatment of esophageal dysmotility secondary to diabetes. He had also been very depressed.

We have given these examples to indicate the degree of certainty and uncertainty surrounding the labels we have applied. While observing due caution, we believe we may offer several observations based on these data. First, when compared to the causes of death observed among people 65 and above at Many Farms from 1957 to 1961 (Table 6.9), myocardial infarctions account for a higher proportion of deaths (five definite and five probable), a possible indication that ischemic heart disease is becoming more common among Navajos. Second, auto accidents continue to be an important cause of death among men in this age group, as they are among younger men. Among the older men in our sample, however, these deaths are the result of having been struck by a motor vehicle. At least one of these men was almost certainly drunk when he was hit as he crossed a road. Third, respiratory failure secondary to tuberculosis is a significant contributing or underlying cause of death but will probably diminish because active tuberculosis has diminished very markedly over the last four decades. Finally, renal failure caused by diabetes is a problem that will almost certainly become more significant because there is some evidence that the incidence of diabetes is increasing among Navajos, as it is among many other Indian populations.

Cause of death among the elderly is related to the question of selection of especially fit people through the filter of high mortality among the young. The selection hypothesis would be particularly convincing if people died young of the same diseases that are important among the elderly (Wing et al. 1985). Thus, if the high rate of young adult mortality was accounted for by heart disease, and if no one with heart disease survived beyond age 65, then of course heart disease would not be a cause of death among the elderly. But it is accidents that account for the excess of mortality of the young, not heart disease. One might argue that the people who die young of accidents include a disproportionate number who, had they lived, would have died of cardiovascular disease and cancer, the diseases of the elderly that seem to be rare among Navajos, but it is difficult to make a convincing case for this possibility in the absence of adequate data on the psychosocial and physiological characteristics of accident victims.

In addition, as we note in chapter 3, rough measures of function indicate that the health status of our sample of Navajos is not significantly different from that of a sample of the Massachusetts population of the same age. By these criteria, then, high mortality at young ages has not resulted in an especially fit older population. A puzzle remains, however, that we shall have to leave unresolved. Surely lower mortality among elderly Navajos is some reflection of better health than is observed in more affluent populations. Unfortunately, we have no comparative data on the prevalence of morbidity other than the few measures of function discussed in chapter 3. Thus we can only suggest that serious classifiable disease entities may well be less common in our sample than in more affluent populations that have lower mortality at young ages. The Navajos' low rates of death from cancer and ischemic heart disease lend some support to this possibility.

Though we believe that the lower death rate of elderly Navajos as compared with the non-Indian population probably does reflect a lesser burden of life-threatening illness, it does not seem to reflect better health as measured by an ability to carry on the tasks of daily living. Several processes seem to be causing the patterns we have observed. First, there does seem to be a selection process at work among men such that they develop more serious illness earlier and die at a younger age than women. Second, the most significant relationship for men appears to be with a wife. Women seem to have a larger number of significant relationships than men. Combined with their generally better health, women are at lower risk of death than men. Thus, when women's health does begin to fail, so many of them are unmarried that marital status is not likely to be predictive of death, and they are more likely to be embedded in social relationships than men so that being unmarried is less of a risk factor in any event. This explanation is not too different from the one suggested for the patterns observed in other populations (Verbrugge 1985). It has been said, for example, that American women have larger numbers of intimate friends than men and are thus protected from the impact of the loss of a spouse.

But there is more to the issue than this. The observation that the most isolated Navajo men also seem to be the ones most likely to have histories of alcohol abuse leads us to ask whether alcohol abuse is a cause of both isolation and physical deterioration, a reaction to isolation and a cause of physical deterioration, or for some people a cause and for others an effect of isolation. What data we have suggest it is both a cause and an effect of isolation. This is an important question to explore further because it raises the very real possibility that in those populations among whom isolation (however measured) is found to be associated with an increased risk of death, it may not be isolation per se that is important but some characteristic of the individual that causes him or her to be both isolated and at increased risk of premature death. If our work is an example, some of the most important determinants—alcohol abuse, for instance—may not have been searched for carefully enough and thus may lead one to conclude, perhaps wrongly, that social isolation is an important cause of an increased risk of death whereas it may turn out in some instances to be simply an epiphenomenon.

Finally, we return to the issue of morbidity among the elderly. It is important to emphasize that high mortality at young ages does not insure the survival of an especially "fit" elderly population. The simple fact that mortality rates are low and may reflect low prevalence and incidence rates of many life-threatening diseases should not be interpreted as meaning that elderly Navajos do not require health and social services. The fact that measures of dysfunction are similar to those observed in other populations whereas poverty is far more common means that people clearly have a great need for various forms of assistance, some of which can be provided by family and friends but many of which cannot.

Navajo disease patterns have changed rapidly since World War II. There is every reason to expect they will continue to change, particularly as ischemic heart disease and diabetes and its complications become more prevalent. Thus we suspect that in not too many more years the low mortality rates that have been common among elderly Navajos will begin to increase, and the kinds of services for which there has not been much demand will become ever more necessary.

►► 7 ◄◄

PERSPECTIVES ON CARING FOR THE ELDERLY

SINCE THE MID-1950S, when the responsibility for Indian health was transferred from the Bureau of Indian Affairs to the U.S. Public Health Service, the quality and accessibility of acute care has improved considerably. The health problems confronting Indians in those early years were still primarily acute infectious diseases of infants and children, and the system that was organized to deal with them was for the most part well designed to do the job. Over the past thirty years, however, disease patterns have changed dramatically (Kunitz 1983). As a result, new conditions are achieving prominence, conditions for which the health and social-service systems are not well suited. These have to do with behavioral and social problems such as accidents and alcohol abuse, as well as chronic diseases and psychosocial problems of the elderly. Such conditions raise in stark form the question of what constitutes a health problem. This is not simply a philosophical issue. Profound policy choices depend on the answer. For example, were the Public Health Service to define the need for custodial care of elderly Navajos as a health problem, a case could be made for converting unfilled acute care beds in Indian Health Service hospitals (where occupancy rates are often 60 to 70 percent) to extended care beds. There is nothing intrinsic to the definition of a health problem that makes such a decision impossible. Such definitions are the result of ethical, political, and economic considerations at least as much as they are the result of "scientific" deliberations.

We raise this issue because it underlies many of the difficulties faced by the elderly—non-Indian as well as Indian, affluent as well as poor—in the United States. As we have said, the Indian Health Service has generally provided accessible, quality acute medical care for at least a generation on most Indian reservations. Likewise, Medicare generally pays promptly for acute hospital admissions of the elderly elsewhere in the nation. What neither of these federal programs is mandated or equipped to do is assume responsibility for chronic supportive care either within institutions or at home.

This chapter describes the provisions that do exist for the care of elderly reservation Navajos and the bureaucratic tangles that have developed as a consequence of the inability of one agency to assume responsibility for the problems of the Indian elderly in the same fashion as acute health care problems have been managed.

HEALTH CARE OF AMERICAN INDIANS

The special relationship "recognized" tribes have with the federal government—of which health and social services are but two examples—is complicated by their relationship to the states in which they reside. Of particular concern here is the role of the states in administering federally funded programs and the eligibility of Indians to participate in state social welfare programs, which may also receive some federal monies (NICOA 1980a; Estes and Lee 1985:23–24). Changes in the federal government's relationship with Indians have tended to contribute to problems in defining state-tribal relationships. There have been some attempts to terminate the special federal trust responsibilities for tribes, which would ultimately result in the extension of state jurisdiction. The support of the sovereign rights of Indian tribes, however, has been sustained as a recognized federal obligation.

Health and social service programs on reservations are largely federally funded. In the past, program priorities and content were generally determined by the Bureau of Indian Affairs (BIA) and the Indian Health Service (IHS). In 1975 the picture was made more complex by the passage of Public Law (PL) 93-638, the Indian Self-Determination and Educational Assistance Act, which allowed tribal governments themselves to undertake many aspects of education and health care program management and delivery of services. Under the provisions of the act, various tribal government departments responsible for health and social services negotiate budget requirements and contracts with the BIA and the IHS, specifying the services they will provide. If approved, federal funds are allocated by the BIA and the IHS through the contracts with the tribes. It then becomes the responsibility of each tribal department to see that these services are provided as described and within the negotiated budgets. Should the cost of program operations exceed the budget, tribes may have to provide interim funds from their own revenues to keep programs running in the short term, but reimbursement from federal agencies for services they are obligated by law to support is expected to be part of the contract procedures.

Aside from purporting to increase Indian "self-determination," this legislation was also prompted by the move to further the decentralization of BIA and IHS operations in accordance with the philosophy of the New Federalism,[1] which sought to transfer more responsibility from the federal to state and local administrative levels (Estes 1979; Estes and Lee 1985:24). Ostensibly, such a national policy of decentralization of health and social services would allow greater sensitivity to regional differences in needs. But it would also shift greater fiscal responsibility to state and local levels, which are most vulnerable to fluctuations in available revenues (Thurow 1985:611). Thus the vagaries of state and local priorities and financing capabilities mean many social programs have become fragmented and eligibility criteria have varied.

A study of the BIA's programs on the reservation, conducted after the push for decentralization began, reported that service provision was being compromised and costs inflated due to a lack of policy and administrative coordination with other federal and state or tribal agencies. Further, across the Navajo reservation as a whole, "the enormous lack of uniformity in program operation between the different [BIA] offices results in programs . . . as varied as possibly could be imagined. Each implements services according to their own interpretation . . . with disparities in service delivery which are so great that basic levels of entitlement may be threatened" (Nass 1980:2).

The situation for the IHS is not much different, particularly with regard to programs for the elderly. At the time of our survey there were no central records of the number of people the IHS had referred to or placed in institutional care facilities on- or off-reservation. Even at the local IHS service unit levels, the availability of such information was extremely variable, leading one administrator to observe that the ability to plan and provide appropriate services for the Navajo elderly under such circumstances was clearly diminished (IHS administrator, personal communication).

Many of these problems are not very different in principle from those facing non-Indian communities. They are complicated beyond recognition, however, by Indians' special legal status and poverty.

Federal Programs and the Indian Elderly

The Administration on Aging (AoA) within the Department of Health and Human Services is the principal federal agency involved in identifying the concerns and needs of the elderly and coordinating available federal resources to meet them (Estes 1979:231). The AoA administers the Older Americans Act of 1965, which established formula grants to state agencies. These grants fund local Agencies on Aging to assist the elderly within their communities by managing and planning the delivery of several social and nutritional services.

In a 1978 amendment to the Older Americans Act, the AoA was authorized to provide tribal organizations with direct grants to finance social and nutritional services for elderly Indians (NICOA 1980b:16). Prior to this, federal funding had been channeled to state agencies, which designated the organizations and programs qualified to receive the funds and provide services. The eligibility requirements established for these state programs resulted in restrictions on the availability of such funds for reservation-based services, and states were not specifically accountable for the proportion of the monies that was being spent on the Indian elderly.[2]

Another significant law is the Indian Health Care Improvement Act (PL 94-437), passed in 1976, and amended in 1980. This law is particularly important with respect to state licensing of tribal nursing homes. It includes an amendment to the Social Security Act that allows IHS hospitals and certain nursing home facilities to qualify for reimbursement under the federal Medicare and Medicaid programs (NICOA 1981c:32). Previously, IHS facilities were not eligible for such compensation because the Social Security Act stipulated that Medicare and Medicaid could not be paid to any provider of services already receiving *federal* monies through other funding channels. Nursing homes in particular receive considerable support from the Medicare and Medicaid programs, and this additional source of funds to Indian health facilities (including hospitals) would be of major importance for reservation populations, who often live in areas remote from other providers of health care. Under this law, facilities are now eligible for Medicare and Medicaid reimbursement whether they are operated by the IHS or by a tribe or tribal organization.

To qualify for such compensation, however, participating facilities must meet the same conditions and requirements as other Medicare and Medicaid facilities. Since many IHS facilities did not initially meet these standards, Congress provided a one-year grace period for facilities that submitted acceptable plans for complying with the regulations (NICOA 1981c:34). The issue of whether eligibility requirements included acquiring state or local licensing for federal (IHS) or tribal facilities located on federal trust lands was left ambiguous (NICOA 1981c:1–3).

A distinction is made between nursing homes that qualify as "skilled care" facilities, which serve the most severely ill and which are eligible for reimbursement under both the Medicare and Medicaid programs, and "intermediate care" facilities, which are eligible only for Medicaid payments. Because state authority in licensing is vague, no specific guidelines are applicable, the standards or criteria applied appear to fluctuate, and tribes are not in a position to develop their own operational standards.

Policy at the State Level

Federal policy over the past decade has required that both the IHS and the BIA take steps to limit their fiscal involvement in the provision of health and social services on the Navajo Reservation, particularly in the area of long-term care (Pritzlaff Commission 1984:8). The Bureau of Indian Affairs has maintained that whether Indians live on- or off-reservation, states have the same responsibilities to provide them with social services as they do to other citizens. From the perspective of the federal government, the responsibility of the BIA and the IHS to Indians is as *residual* resources for services that are not available through state or local programs, where the major responsibility should, in fact, be retained (NICOA 1980a:7).

Federal agencies responsible for administering federal Indian policy, however, often depend on state and local governments for the actual distribution of services. This situation has been perpetuated through modifications made in 1983 to Title XX of the Social Security Act, which supplies federal block grants (Social Service Block Grants, or SSBGs) to states to provide a variety of social services. Again, the intention was to give states more discretion in developing services, but as with other programs administered in this fashion, eligibility criteria vary not only among the states but in some cases among the counties of individual states (Estes and Lee 1985:24, 31; Johnson and Grant 1985:163; McCall 1985:xiv–38).

The Navajo Reservation covers portions of three states, and different procedures must be followed to obtain services in each. In Arizona, a certain proportion of Title XX monies is designated for distribution to Indian tribes according to their population. Local communities on the Navajo Reservation submit budget proposals for using Title XX funds to the tribal Division of Social Welfare. New Mexico, in contrast, awards Title XX funds strictly on the basis of program proposals. In their attempts to design programs to serve reservation elderly, tribes often have to compete for funds with other local government agencies and with private organizations. Under such circumstances, tribal priorities may have to be subordinated to those set by a state or federal agency. Navajos living on a small section of the reservation in Utah decided to deal directly with the state through county offices rather than through the tribe.

State and local governments have varied in their willingness to cooperate with and work through tribal authorities. Special problems develop where care provision requires judicial and regulatory authorization (NICOA 1981c). For example, in cases involving the commitment of mentally incompetent persons or the licensing of nursing homes or long-term care facilities on a reservation, the states have been unwilling to give recognition to tribal courts and authorities (NICOA 1980a:23).

Inconsistencies in funding and licensing procedures for on- and off-reservation long-term care facilities illustrate how variations in state policies influence the availability of services for the Navajo elderly. Nationwide, the cost of medical care for the indigent is generally shared by the federal and state governments through the Medicaid program. In 1976, when the Indian Health Care Improvement Act went into effect, Medicaid and Medicare funds became available to tribally operated facilities. Alone among the states, Arizona (where the majority of Navajos live) chose not to participate in the Medicaid program, forcing its counties to assume the major responsibility for indigent health care. When this proved financially impossible, Arizona developed the Arizona Health Care Cost Containment System (AHCCCS) as a demonstration project of the federal Health Care Financing Administration (HCFA) to provide acute-care health service to the indigent in the state (McCall 1985:xv–29).

In order to simplify the initial bidding process for administering and implementing the AHCCCS program, both Native Americans and nursing home residents were omitted from the original Request for Proposal (RFP). The state feared that taking on prepayment of long-term care services would dilute any savings that might be realized in the area of acute-care services. After the legislation passed, the state determined that an otherwise eligible individual could not be denied services solely on the basis of residence (i.e., a nursing home). But the state has continued to exclude the major responsibility for long-term care services from the AHCCCS program, creating considerable administrative complexity as the state and the counties attempt to pass the financial burden back and forth, and great disparities in services provided (McCall 1985:xv–3, 10, 21; xiv–39, 45).

During 1982, the first year AHCCCS was in operation, a special RFP was issued to include services to Indians eligible for AHCCCS programs, but contract documents were never implemented. Although an emergency regulation was adopted the following year, the methods of reimbursement involving the IHS, the AHCCCS, and the counties were unclear and complicated. As a result, non-reservation-based physicians were reluctant to provide medical services to Indians when it was uncertain how and whether they would be reimbursed (McCall 1985:vi–14).

In 1984 the state of Arizona took over the administration of AHCCCS from the initial subcontractor because of management problems and revenue losses. AHCCCS nursing home care coverage remains restricted to medical services for a limited period following a patient's admission, after which the counties bear most of the financial responsibility for indigent long-term care costs. As a result, such services remain fragmentary and minimal, and eligibility regulations across counties have not been standardized (McCall 1985:xiv–38).[3]

In neighboring states, completely different administrative policies are in effect. Therefore, elderly Navajos may be either better or worse off, depending on where they happen to reside on the reservation. Further, the tribal government is restricted in its jurisdictional and financial ability to overcome local variations in service availability.

Tribal Governments and Health Policy

Many people viewed the Indian Self-Determination Act (PL 93-638) as a mechanism for increasing the role of tribal governments in the provision of health and social services on reservations. Unfortunately, its impact has fallen short of tribal expectations, and it has intensified internal competition for, and dependence on, federal funding. Within tribal administrations, management responsibilities for social service problems have become the major focus of political attention (Guillemin 1980). As a result, "cadres of tribal grantsmen . . . have been created . . . with personal and bureaucratic ties to a variety of federal agencies on which continuing support depends" (Kunitz 1983:48; see also Levy and Kunitz 1981). Further, longtime Navajo employees of the BIA and IHS, the agencies that administer the distribution of PL 93-638 monies, may be placed in an adversarial relationship with people in tribal government programs who are attempting to obtain access to these funds.

Some tribal leaders foresaw these and other negative repercussions and therefore decided against entering into contractual agreements with the federal government to administer programs. Of particular concern was whether PL 93-638 contracts would include provisions for inflation when program budgets were established. If not, the actual amount of funds available would quickly decline. This situation would be exacerbated by the fact that administrative expenses for the usually isolated tribal governments are higher than for federal agencies, and one provision of the Self-Determination Act was that programs taken over by the tribes must provide services comparable to those previously available (Kunitz 1983:48). Ultimately, in order for an insufficiently funded program to be continued throughout a contract period, tribes would be placed in the position of having to redistribute their own restricted revenues to cover the deficits.

One consequence of the Self-Determination Act's budgetary policies on the Navajo Reservation has been an intensification of intratribal antagonisms over health service priorities. The underfunding of contracts has often required frenzied last-minute shifts of tribal money from other programs, followed by a reduction in services and a loss of jobs. Another catch in the contracting process involving PL 93-638 funds has been that, while fiscal management and program maintenance responsibilities may reside in the tribal governments, other aspects of policy-making may not. For example, the Navajo Tribe has wanted to establish a number of community-based group homes for the elderly in need of only personal care. The tribe contracted with the BIA, through self-determination monies, to develop several of these facilities. Because federal funds were being used, however, the tribe itself did not have the authority to determine who was eligible to receive care in the group homes.

The BIA's position, based on contractual regulations, is that if an elderly person has income above a certain level, he or she is ineligible for certain programs supported by PL 93-638 funds. As a result, some individuals who receive Supplemental Security Income (SSI) payments (because their assets are below federal poverty levels) or Navajo tribal welfare assistance supplements (under the General Assistance program) are considered to have income above that allowed for clients eligible for admission to the group homes. In other cases, a waiver of the PL 93-638 CFR has been implemented. The waiver states that when a person requires high-cost or high-level custodial care, SSI does not make the client ineligible for nursing care services, although such income is used to offset the cost of patient care. This often occurs for clients at the reservation's two institutional nursing care facilities.

In both tribal and federal service agencies there was disagreement about the circumstances under which this waiver was applicable. Such income limitations were generally considered unrealistically restrictive, and the regulations were seen as undermining, in many cases, the capacity to develop noninstitutional care service for the elderly—supposedly a goal of both tribal and federal governments. Specifically, certain types of community and in-home services that do not approach the around-the-clock care and board available through institutional facilities are not included within this waiver. The Senior Companion Program (SCP), for example, offers from one to five hours a week of in-home light housekeeping and personal care assistance. An elderly applicant, however, may be considered ineligible if he or she receives SSI. Federal guidelines for Action programs, with which the SCP is affiliated, set the cut-off for income eligibility at the poverty level *plus* SSI benefits. As restrictive as Arizona's regulations are, the state recognizes that people who qualify for SSI benefits do so because of insufficient income, and such individuals by definition qualify for a series of social services. Only tribal programs supported by PL 93-638 subcontract funds from the BIA use SSI itself as a criterion indicating an income sufficient to make some recipients ineligible to receive services. The Navajo Tribe is engaging in a legal suit against the BIA to try to obtain authority to set their own eligibility standards for programs the tribe administers with self-determination funds.

Further, since 1981, when it took over the provision of social services from the BIA (through PL 93-638 contracts), the Navajo tribe has argued that these programs have been consistently underfunded. The ensuing debate over how to acquire necessary financial support before the beginning of a new contract period has left many programs financially uncertain from one month to the next. Since providing these services is a federal responsibility, the tribal administration is to be reimbursed for funds that it had to expend to cover these deficits. As of mid-1984, however, the Navajo Tribe had not received any such compensation. In fact, there was heated debate over whether the contract for service provision should be returned to the BIA in order to avoid a further, and what some perceived as an intentional, exploitation of tribal revenues.[4]

THE NAVAJO ELDERLY

As noted earlier, disease patterns have changed dramatically on the Navajo Reservation, with much lower infant and maternal mortality rates and a decreased incidence of infectious disease (Kunitz 1983:82, 86). Twenty years ago, when infant and child malnutrition was a greater problem, these age groups were the focus of health improvement concerns. With a simultaneous push to educate young people as a means of bettering the condition of the tribe generally, Navajo youth became targeted as the "hope for the future." As disease patterns changed, pediatric problems decreased and hospital beds began to be filled more often by elderly patients. In addition, as the proportion of elderly in the overall U.S. population increased, policies were initiated that expanded social services for them at the federal level. Similar priorities developed in the early 1970s on the Navajo Reservation. Before that time, no tribal aging program existed. In contrast, the Navajo tribal chairman designated 1981 as the Year of the Elderly, with the stated goal that the tribal administration's Aging Services Department should "develop a support system that will keep you . . . [the elderly] in your own community and in your own homes" (NTCOA 1981:vi).

Social Service and Health Care for Navajo Elderly

The earliest programs targeted specifically at Navajo elderly were senior centers and congregate meal sites. These were initially organized in the late 1970s and early 1980s in the eastern sections of the reservation near the tribal administrative headquarters and were under the guidance of a VISTA worker familiar with the programs authorized by the Older Americans Act. The First National Indian Conference on Aging in 1976 highlighted the concern that the interests of the Indian elderly were not being adequately represented within the growing national movement to focus attention on the needs of older Americans (NICOA 1976).

Another major policy concern in the 1970s was aimed at returning to the reservation as many Navajos of all ages as possible who were hospitalized or institutionalized in Phoenix, Albuquerque, or other distant (250–400 miles) urban centers. Employees of both the BIA and several tribal organizations claim to have initiated this "return to the reservation" movement. It became fraught with strong emotional overtones and was aimed mainly at improving the Navajo patients' quality of life. Some observers noted that the BIA initiated a major campaign to return all its off-reservation placements just as it was turning over responsibility for service provision to the Navajo Tribe and that the BIA had initiated little in the way of a planned, formal policy to assess the feasibility of handling these clients locally. Problems existed regarding the lack of adequate facilities on the reservation to accommodate the needs of some of these people, the expense of providing institutional care, and the fluctuating availability of community-based services as alternatives to nursing homes.

In the late 1970s, when the Navajo Tribe took over the management of many social and health service programs from the BIA and the IHS, a group of tribal departments was organized to coordinate these responsibilities. The Division of Social Welfare (DSW) handles contracts with the BIA to provide social services funded through PL 93-638 funds, and it also manages federal Title XX monies received through state grants.

The Division of Health Improvement Services (DHIS) was the tribe's first health department. It develops and operates a variety of community health and social service programs across the reservation with a preventive health focus. DHIS includes the Navajo Aging Services departments, with several programs (e.g., Elderly Group Homes and the Senior Companion Program), receiving at least partial funding from PL 93-638 funds through the Division of Social Welfare. Although initially the only PL 93-638 funds the DHIS received directly were for management development projects, in the future it may seek to contract directly with the BIA for service provision funds as well. The

DHIS also includes a Preventive Health Department, which administers the Community Health Representative and Home Health programs, among others.

On-Reservation Institutional Facilities

The desire to return American Indian elderly to their home areas resulted in the push to construct nursing homes on reservations, where clients would be close to their families, and to staff them with Indians from their own tribes (Levy 1967:235; Mick 1983:7). The first Indian Nursing Home was built in 1969; the others were built during the 1970s. As of 1983 there were eight nursing homes on Indian reservations in this country. Two of them, serving different care levels, are located on the Navajo Reservation. Prior to their construction, most Navajo elderly requiring nursing home care were sent to Phoenix or Albuquerque, and even now the 145-bed capacity of these two facilities is not adequate to meet the tribe's needs.

Medicare reimbursement for institutional long-term care services is available to those meeting the federal qualifications. But since many elderly Indians were not employed long enough in steady wage-work positions, few are eligible. Further, Medicare is very limited in the type and extent of nursing home care it will cover.

There are different care levels for which nursing homes are licensed to handle patients, with the major distinction being between skilled and intermediate care facilities. The standards for the two care levels are very similar; the basic difference is in requirements for professional staffing. Intermediate care specifications for nursing and physician services are less rigorous, and continual medical direction by a physician is not required (Johnson and Grant 1985:177).

The one "skilled" care facility on the Navajo Reservation is located in the town of Chinle and has a continual 95 to 100 percent occupancy rate. It opened in 1971, and it has about 29 beds available for skilled care patients and another 40 for intermediate care patients. The Chinle facility was established and managed by a nonprofit charitable organization until it went bankrupt in 1978. It is now managed by the Navajo Tribe, and contracts from the IHS and the tribal DSW are its current sources of support. It is called the Chinle Extended Care Facility to indicate that it is intended as a facility to serve all age groups, not just the elderly. In 1984, 75 percent of Chinle's patient population was over 65. About half of the skilled care patients and 85 percent of the intermediate care patients were in that age group. Most patients were from the eastern half of the reservation, and health service administrators from the western areas often stated that they could rarely get referrals accepted into this facility because it favored the eastern section.

One individual from our random sample was at the Chinle care center when we began our project. There had been no openings there when her application was first submitted. She subsequently spent ten months in an IHS contract care facility at Phoenix awaiting admission at Chinle. Tribal social service personnel told us that such delays, let alone off-reservation interim arrangements, are rare at present and that efforts are made to find relatives to care for the client until nursing home placement is available. Most people agreed that placements at distances as far as Phoenix are unusual, but waiting periods of six months to a year are reportedly not uncommon. At the time of our interview, another family was attempting to have their mother admitted and eventually succeeded about three months later. They claimed, however, that they had initiated several unsuccessful attempts over the previous two to three years.

There have been continuous licensing disputes between the Chinle facility, the state, and the IHS, as well as funding negotiations with the tribe. The complex problem of acquiring adequate and consistent funding created an embattled atmosphere for Chinle's administrative staff. Due in part to its isolated location, with the associated increased cost of acquiring supplies and services, the Chinle facility's patient care fees are higher than off-reservation nursing homes (as of June 1984, Chinle's fees were about to be raised to $100 a day from $60 to $70 a day). The IHS pays only for patients at skilled care levels, while others are considered the financial responsibility of the tribe. Since Chinle is in Arizona, no Medicaid funds are available for intermediate care patients.

The IHS is attempting to reduce its own budget expenditures, provoking claims that the degree of a person's health problems is downgraded in order to decrease the financial liability of the IHS. However, this possible downgrading would also affect a patient's eligibility for Medicare reimbursement. Ironically, if the IHS will not cover the cost of skilled care for a patient at the Chinle facility, the same patient might have been cared for as an inpatient at the IHS hospital for a fee of $250 a day. On the other hand, the IHS contends that the Chinle facility tends to exaggerate the level of its patients' health problems and that it is less expensive to place them off-reservation, where the IHS has service contracts with extended care facilities. Due to budget limitations and increasing patient care costs, the IHS claims it cannot afford to pay for skilled care services at the Chinle facility, where more effective management policies might help lower costs to levels more competitive with the off-reservation contract facilities.

At the time of our study, the Chinle facility was Medicare certified and should have been reimbursed for the care of certain skilled care patients. Chinle staff members blamed the cumbersome paperwork process for ongoing reimbursement delays, which were particularly threatening, since funding for the facility was generally so precarious, causing a continual cash-flow problem.

The licensing and care-level definitional problems have created considerable administrative problems for the Chinle facility, and in fact its Arizona state license had expired six months before we began our work there. Previously, the IHS had sent a team to review the nursing home's qualifications for state licensing, but it had recently decided that since the Chinle facility is on federal land, it does not *require* state licensing. Should the Chinle program want to acquire state certification, the facility must arrange and pay for the process itself, thus stretching an already precarious budget even thinner. The IHS is now concerned solely with obtaining Medicare certification, since this makes monies available for patients requiring skilled care, patients for whom the IHS would no longer be responsible. The Chinle facility's administration noted that while the state of Arizona has specific written guidelines for classifying a patient at the skilled care level, Medicare procedures provide more general criteria. Hence, problems that qualify for skilled care services vary for each patient and differ from diagnosis to diagnosis. From the perspective of the Chinle Extended Care Facility, it would be preferable to have stricter state guidelines followed in order to allow for less arbitrary decisions about which patients are eligible for IHS financial support.

The Navajo tribal government's attitude toward nursing homes also influences funding available for facilities on the reservation. Both reservation institutional facilities are in Arizona, and the tribal Division of Social Welfare is responsible for paying service costs for less than skilled care patients through PL 93-638 monies. These funds were not being allocated for construction (neither the IHS nor the BIA budgets included money for the construction of facilities) or maintenance and upkeep costs of the nursing care facilities, yet when they are evaluated and considered for licensing, general building conditions are often criticized.[5]

The Navajo Tribe's Council on Aging is reportedly more supportive of the tribal Aging Department's group home program than of nursing homes, but the levels of care these programs offer differ considerably. Generally the nursing homes are less favored because of the council's position that it is the younger generation's responsibility to care for their own elderly family members. This is similar to the push for deinstitutionalization advocated at the national level. Institutional staff noted, however, that there are cases in which the elderly have health problems that simply cannot be handled in a family setting. On the other hand, BIA administrators argued that Chinle was established to serve mainly as a skilled care facility, and while intermediate or custodial care elderly ("easy clients") may require less costly services, the facility's greater emphasis on serving these patients over the severely ill of all age groups means its mandate is not being fulfilled. They believe, therefore, that intermediate or custodial care patients should be cared for at home or in other facilities, leaving Chinle to provide the skilled services for which it was intended. The contradictions inherent in the differing perspectives of the IHS, the BIA, tribal program administrators, and Chinle facility managers are grounded in attempts to meet divergent service needs with conflicting funding limitations and overlapping jurisdictional authorities.

While the two individuals from our sample who were admitted to the Chinle Extended Care Facility both had children and other relatives living nearby, adequate care was not available outside of the institution. In the first case, Mrs. Ason (a pseudonym) had had a stroke about four years prior to our interview that left her partially paralyzed and unable to speak. Although she fed herself, Mrs. Ason required aid in moving, dressing, bathing, and using the bathroom. One daughter had cared for her mother for several years until the birth of her two youngest children created unmanageable crowding and care responsibilities. Most recently, Mrs. Ason had been living with another, newly divorced daughter but was at times verbally and physically abusive to her adolescent grandchildren. Further, her daughter was working full-time, and consistent day care was difficult to obtain. For a while another daughter (with whom we conducted our interview) came during the day to care for Mrs. Ason, but this daughter had severe health problems of her own and several children to care for as well, including one who was paraplegic. There were no other relatives available or willing to provide the level of care Mrs. Ason required on a full-time basis, especially since her monthly social security check barely covered her needs for food, special shoes and soaps, and diapers.

Records from the Chinle facility indicate that for the first six weeks after admission, Mrs. Ason was sometimes hostile toward other residents and was not very communicative. But she was visited about every two weeks by family and friends, which made a considerable difference in her general mood. By the third month, Mrs. Ason's hostile behavior had ended, she was taking part in group activities, and reportedly she had adjusted well to the care facility environment. While Mrs. Ason's relatives, especially her granddaughters, regretted having to send her as far away as Chinle, family relations and some members' health were crumbling under the weight of four years of the daily intensive care Mrs. Ason required. The family anticipated having the resources to visit Mrs. Ason, and they evidently made the 260-mile round-trip between Tuba City and Chinle regularly. They believed Mrs. Ason was being well cared for at the nursing home and in a manner that the family was unable to provide.

A second woman from our sample, Mrs. Tso (a pseudonym), had been a resident at Chinle Extended Care for about a year prior to our interview with her at the facility. She also had multiple health problems, including diabetes and loss of sight in one eye due to cataracts. However, her most debilitating problems stemmed from a hip fracture, as a result of which she required constant assistance with daily activities. Mrs. Tso was very overweight, and the fracture had never healed properly. Her husband had died more than 20 years before, and she had maintained good relations with only one of her five children over the years. This daughter had lived next door in Tuba City and acted as her mother's home caretaker for an extended period. When the daughter's husband died and she developed health problems of her own, she could no longer provide her mother with adequate constant care. Through IHS and tribal programs, several home care workers were assigned to Mrs. Tso, but her size made caring for her physically difficult, and she was often a far-from-cooperative client. One worker was unable to reconcile the need to be firm in keeping Mrs. Tso on her medication schedule with the fact that she was an elderly clan relative, a relationship demanding respect. Like others before her, this caretaker requested a transfer to another case.

Mrs. Tso was not an easy person to get along with, yet family relations were further strained because she adhered steadfastly to traditional Navajo religious beliefs (her father had been a ceremonialist, and Mrs. Tso was an herbalist and hand trembler), while several of her children became Christians. This created insurmountable rifts among some family members. Mrs. Tso herself decided she needed institutional care even though she recognized that the one daughter she was close to had no vehicle. In fact, when we spoke with Mrs. Tso, her daughter had been able to visit her only twice over the previous year. Mrs. Tso seemed to have adjusted fairly well to her life at the Chinle facility, reportedly interacting with other residents, handling her own finances, and occasionally sewing and selling pillows. However, she reported to us that since entering the Chinle facility she had begun, for the first time in her life, to have periods from two to three days at a time when she felt despondent and lonely. This occurred once or twice each month, but she said that when she went and talked to someone on the staff, it usually made her feel better. While residence in the Chinle facility was not an ideal situation, Mrs. Tso herself acknowledged that there were no alternatives, given her health and family situation. Ironically, in the last year of her life, Mrs. Tso became more accepting of Christianity. She died of a stroke only a few weeks after we spoke with her.

In both these cases the elderly individuals had been living in Tuba City for an extended period, and their families did not have a traditional land use area around which economic and social life was oriented. Their children's families all lived separately and sometimes quite a distance apart, many just managing to handle their own individual needs without the extra time or resources to care for their elderly relative. In these cases, neither the families nor the elderly themselves objected strongly to the institutional setting itself but rather to its distance from their local community. On the other hand, some of our respondents were afraid of the prospect of being sent to a nursing home. One woman extrapolated from her experience while working as a Senior Companion in the Tuba City hospital to what she expected life would be like in such a place. Although disturbed by the lack of intimacy between staff and elderly patients, and the infrequency with which family members visited, she was most concerned about being sent from her home in Tuba City to a "strange place" like Chinle.

The other institutional care center on the Navajo Reservation, located at Toyei, has 66 available beds with only 1 vacant at the time of our survey. While it is about 40 miles closer to Tuba City in terms of highway travel distance, Toyei is a very small and isolated community that contrasts dramatically with Chinle, one of the largest towns on the Navajo Reservation. Families visiting relatives at Chinle Extended Care can do weekly shopping, laundry, and other errands while in town. None of these options exist in Toyei. Because there are few paved roads on the reservation, most people own trucks, which are hardly fuel efficient. Gasoline is extremely expensive locally, and most people simply cannot afford to travel long distances for the luxury of a visit with relatives.

In 1978 the old Toyei boarding school was renovated with voluntary labor and building supplies provided by the BIA and began its operation as a branch of Chinle Extended Care. Toyei was intended specifically for the care of the elderly (intermediate and custodial levels only) because the Chinle facility could not handle the patient load resulting from the push to return the elderly from off-reservation nursing homes. However, the tribal Department of Social Welfare also referred younger mentally retarded patients to Toyei as temporary residents because there was nowhere else on the reservation to house them. In 1985 about 15 percent of the current clients fell into this category.

Toyei is 26 miles from the IHS hospital on the Hopi Reservation and 22 miles from a private hospital in Ganado. Occasionally Toyei patients are taken to these facilities, because the nearest IHS hospital in the same administrative region is about 65 miles east at Fort Defiance. Both Toyei and Chinle experience difficulty recruiting and keeping qualified employees. Only a few individuals, recruited through either Salt Lake City or a Boston-based employment pool, have held permanent nursing positions for more than a few months. While available salaries are generally competitive with other areas, the isolation and unfamiliar cultural setting often require too great an adjustment. There are not enough trained Navajo nurses to fill the needs of these facilities.

Toyei staff cited budgetary problems similar to those experienced at the Chinle facility, emphasizing the difficulty of negotiating adequate rate increases. Due to PL 93-638 contract regulations, both facilities are reimbursed after services are provided. Thus, patients are cared for and staff payrolls disbursed before funds covering the current pay periods are actually received. While at present Toyei is completely dependent on PL 93-638 monies, its administration is exploring other, less restricted sources of funding. One stumbling block is the stipulation that currently available PL 93-638 funds should be used for basics like food costs and direct health maintenance expenses rather than for facility improvements. However, Toyei is located in an open, isolated, and extremely sparsely populated area, and fencing is needed because during pervious winters (the elevation in this area of the reservation is about 5,000 feet) patients have wandered off from the facility, and finding them proved very difficult. Since PL 93-638 monies are not available for structural improvements, Toyei has not been able to meet facility certification requirements that would allow it to qualify for private foundation funding.[6]

Because of its remote location and the limited services it can provide, tribal officials are reluctant to invest a great deal of money to renovate Toyei. An alternative would be to build a new structure near an existing hospital. Residents of the western end of the reservation have often suggested that Tuba City would be an appropriate site, because hospital facilities are already available there and because they believe they are underserved by the Chinle and Toyei facilities. Regardless of the fact that these care centers are on the reservation, they are far enough away (about 130 and 90 miles, respectively) that having elderly family members there is not considered to be keeping them in the "local community." Although the immediate cost of building a new structure would be greater than renovating Toyei, there would be more flexibility in the services that could be provided and hence wider eligibility options with respect to funding sources.

Slightly more than half of the clients at Toyei are over 65, and most of these are about 80 years of age. While 56 percent of the clients over age 65 had been admitted within the last two years, 28 percent had been there 5 years, and more than 10 percent had been admitted in 1978 when Toyei first opened. The main reason given for requesting that the elderly client be admitted to Toyei was that the family could not provide required daily custodial care. Staff members indicated that once patients are admitted, most of the time they remain until they die. But clients can go home on visits, and indeed some do return to stay with their families for several weeks at a time over the summer months. From a federal funding perspective, this is considered an inappropriate policy for extended care or group home facilities because they are reimbursed on a "filled bed" basis. A high-ranking state administrator in Arizona's state aging programs insisted that such a use pattern proves the client does have a home setting where care can be provided and that the individual is really not sufficiently ill or disabled to require institutionalization. This perspective ignores the realities of family residence patterns on the reservation.

During summers on the reservation, the weather is mild and children are home from school and available to help care for elderly family members. But winters are harsh in many areas, and dirt roads often become impassable for weeks at a time. The facility at Toyei provides warm shelter, running water, a constant food supply, and attendant care—services often unavailable at the family's homesite. Some elderly have relatives with homes in towns where these services are accessible, and as they become more frail, they have begun to winter with these family members. One of our informants, whose traditional campsite is in a rural area about 10 miles north of Tuba City, described how she always disliked visiting her daughter's house in town because there was a toilet *inside* it. However, due to increasing stiffness and pains in her legs, she is fearful of spending the cold winter months at her traditional camp, where she must negotiate sometimes icy ground when using the outdoor facilities. She is therefore resigned to compromising her sensibilities for safety's sake and spending winters with her daughter. Unfortunately, many Navajo elderly do not have such an option. The need for more flexibility in the types of facility use patterns approved and supported by both federal and tribal agencies, including seasonal residence, has been noted in other reservation settings as well (Rogers and Gallion 1978:487).

About half of Toyei's clients reportedly had only one or no living children and no other relatives able or willing to care for them. The major circumstances contributing to the inability to care for the elderly at home were (1) family employment responsibilities in distant communities or off-reservation, (2) inadequate housing to meet the needs of a frail elderly person, or (3) children or other relatives with financial difficulties and/or drinking problems, with the result that the elderly are left unattended. The staff at Toyei reported that more than 50 percent of their clients were infrequently visited by family members, again due in part to Toyei's isolated location.

In 1979 the IHS estimated that a total of 146 people on the reservation would be in need of skilled care services in the following year (Navajo Health Systems Agency 1981:4a). Even if these figures had not increased by the time of our survey, reservation facilities could only provide beds for 20 percent of these people. A possible alternative to building new structures may be the development of skilled nursing care bed capacity at private and IHS hospitals on the reservation.

Such a use of existing facilities would be less expensive, and services would be available in a shorter period of time. But complex funding arrangements remain to be worked out between the tribe, the IHS, local communities, and hospital management.

Off-Reservation Nursing Homes

Unlike Arizona, New Mexico participates in the Medicaid program, and there are several nursing home facilities located just beyond the eastern boundaries of the Navajo reservation in the towns of Gallup and Farmington, New Mexico. In contrast, until the final months of our study, the closest nursing homes in Arizona to which the IHS would make referrals for Navajo clients and pay for service fees were in Phoenix, several hundred miles to the south. There are now two small nursing homes in Flagstaff, Arizona, about 20 miles from the reservation's southwestern border. However, due in part to funding limitations, there have been only a few Navajo patients at these facilities.

During the summer of 1984, there were about 71 elderly Navajos in the nursing homes in border towns in New Mexico. These clients are mainly supported by Medicaid funds or PL 93-638 subcontracts administered through the Navajo Tribal Division of Social Welfare and are classified at the intermediate/custodial care level. Most are from communities in New Mexico or along the eastern border of Arizona. The state of New Mexico is willing to accept a certain number of Navajo clients from Arizona because of the placement problems in that state, and reciprocal assistance is expected. Once patients are accepted into the New Mexico facility, that is considered their legal residence, but should the burden of handling their own clients become too great, stricter residency regulations would have to be enforced (Russell personal communication, 1984). The tribal social service staff did not consider these to be "off-reservation" placements because many families living in the eastern area of the reservation go to these towns at least weekly to shop or visit relatives, or for other reasons.

A similar survey in Arizona in 1984 located only two elderly Navajos in off-reservation nursing homes. A director of one of the facilities in Phoenix (where clients used to be sent on a regular basis) noted that many former patients had been returned to the reservation in the late 1970s, and admissions were now infrequent. However, he noted that since the tribe still does not have appropriate facilities to serve the severely and/or violent mentally ill, these types of clients continue to be referred to Phoenix for care.

Residential and Community-Based Programs

As noted, a recent priority of Navajo tribal programs for the elderly has been to develop community-based and noninstitutional programs. This follows the change in priorities for aging services nationally from nursing homes as models for long-term care to in-home services. Proponents of this policy argue that costs for care at residential facilities and in the home are less than at large institutions, and the elderly are happier receiving care in more familiar settings. However, one Navajo administrator observed that the tribe never got, nor has it developed, an adequate service base to handle either institutional or community-based and in-home services. Limitations on funding as well as administrative restrictions have also narrowed the options for available services.

Within the tribal bureaucracy, programs serving the elderly are not administered solely by one department, but an unusual attempt has been made within the Division of Health Improvement Services to coordinate and maximize federal and state funding sources through the development of what is called the Navajo Area Agency on Aging. As described earlier, under the auspices of the Older Americans Act, the Administration on Aging set up 50 state units on aging, and within each state various area agencies on aging administer monies for senior citizen centers and other specified programs. Because the Navajo Reservation covers portions of three states, it proved very complex to set up AoA services for elderly Navajos. After several years of negotiations, the governors of all three states agreed to pool portions of their AoA program monies, and since 1979 the reservation, including the sections in Utah and New Mexico, has been administered as a single Tri-State Area Agency on Aging (NTCOA 1981).

The Navajo Area Agency on Aging also works to acquire funds for aging services from other federal, state, and tribal programs. However, the tribal government does not acknowledge it as the sole coordinating division for aging programs on the reservation. Within the large and complex bureaucracy of the Navajo Tribe, there are conflicts in priorities for health planning targeted for the elderly as opposed to other groups. Questions about the development of new facilities, their location, and the level of services to be provided are all continuing sources of debate.

The first community-based services developed specifically for the elderly on the reservation were senior centers. While at present about 60 percent of the local communities on the reservation have such centers, the tribe's goal is to have such facilities available consistently in all areas. They are set up similarly to those sponsored elsewhere by the AoA, with congregate meals served at the facility sites and some home-delivered meal service available. However, transportation costs and the difficulty of travel on the reservation's mostly unpaved roads limits meal delivery to within short distances of the centers. Further, the centers that remain open and provide meals most consistently are those in or near the major towns. Centers in more remote locations are open sporadically as funding and staff availability permit. Until their service provision stabilizes, these centers cannot be considered a realistic community-based resource for the rural elderly.

Group homes were developed to provide emergency, winter and safe housing alternatives for the elderly with the idea of reducing the number of inappropriate institutional placements. They provide residential and nonresidential adult custodial care to eligible clients (usually 6 to 10 per home) who require personal self-care assistance, social support services, and protective services. However, this program is facing serious funding problems because it depends on limited PL 93-638 monies, for which the priority is maintaining nonresidential day-care services.

Two of the facilities are remodeled homes built as residences for BIA employees, while the third is an entirely new residence. All the homes are equipped with safety features specifically for the frail elderly, and they provide regular access to appropriate health care. After adjusting to an initial discomfort about living in such close proximity to strangers (which is especially a problem for some elderly women thrust into a mixed-sex environment), the residents generally had very positive responses to this arrangement. While there is increasing interest in using these facilities as day-care centers for the elderly, there are no easy solutions to the difficulty of transporting clients to these facilities on a daily basis. Their usefulness is limited to those elderly living very nearby. To be widely accessible, similar facilities would need to be available in every local community—an unlikely prospect. In fact, no funds were available to expand the program beyond the three group homes (located at Greasewood, Arizona; Aneth, Utah; and Shiprock, New Mexico) operating in 1984.

Several types of community-based services are available sporadically to the elderly in particular but also to disabled or disadvantaged individuals of all ages. They include housing improvement and/or energy assistance programs. Several of our informants living in Tuba City had been assigned homes in modern tribal housing projects after community service workers evaluated their former residences as inadequate. Since there were no family members available to provide either full-time care or housing, these elderly were at times alone in structures that often had unfamiliar features. After about an hour into an interview with a woman in such circumstances, it seemed extremely warm inside her house although it was a cold midwinter day. When we checked the thermostat, it read 92°, and it turned out that our informant did not know how to regulate the furnace. It also was not unusual to visit rural campsites where tribal assistance programs had built small modern homes or hogans with indoor plumbing fixtures for the elderly. While on the surface they appear to provide improved living conditions, operative water and septic tanks often were not available, so their usefulness was limited. We were interrupted at the end of one interview by workers who had come to connect the plumbing fixtures some four years after our informant's house had been built. In another case, an elderly couple could not afford to have the water service for their indoor plumbing connected.

The modern housing structures were sometimes used mainly for storage, especially during the winter, because the thin wooden plank construction made them difficult and expensive to heat. For some elderly, the cost of hiring someone to bring wood, or of buying gasoline if they could haul wood themselves was prohibitive. Many people maintained their traditional hogan adjacent to the newer structures because the hogans were warmer in winter and cooler in summer. Thus, while community-based assistance programs have had a significant impact for some individuals, their applicability to circumstances across the reservation is often limited, and their availability is always sporadic.

In-Home Care Services

The availability of in-home care services is quite variable across the reservation, building again mainly on a legacy of programs established without uniformity within geographic subunits of the Bureau of Indian Affairs. In the Tuba City and Crownpoint areas, the Adult Foster Care program is operated as a day residential caretaker program in which clients are visited in their homes a certain number of hours per day (never more than eight), and general cleaning, cooking, and personal care services are provided. However, in the Fort Defiance Agency, "foster" families (preferably those of relatives) are paid to care for the elderly person in the foster family's home. This program does not exist in other areas on the reservation.

A similar level of in-home custodial care is available through the Senior Companion Program (SCP), but services to each client are limited to a few hours a week. Also priority conflicts over local funding within the various reservation communities mean that the quality and quantity of these services are variable across the reservation. Income regulations for participants again may designate some elderly receiving SSI as ineligible for needed assistance in situations in which few service alternatives are available. Further, the limited funds available for caretaker transportation expenses make it nearly impossible to assist the elderly who live any distance from the few towns dispersed across the reservation, and substantial outreach programs have received only sporadic funding in the past. A strong positive aspect of this program and the Foster Grandparent Program (FGP) is that they employ (at minimal wages) low-income men and women age 50 years and older (for SCP) or age 60 and older (for FGP) to provide, respectively, service to high-risk elderly and physically or mentally handicapped children. In this way, older Navajos are employed in assisting the elderly, and the elderly themselves are part of significant service programs.

The IHS developed Community Health Representative (CHR) and visiting nurse programs to provide needed health care beyond the town-based hospitals and clinics. Patients of any age who are recovering from an acute illness may, on a physician's orders, be visited temporarily by the nursing outreach services and receive in-home care services. One of our informants, Mrs. Tsosie, is totally blind and has no close relatives willing to take on her care responsibilities. Through this program she is assisted by a home-care worker, a clan relative described as her major support system, for 8 hours a day, 5 days a week. Mrs. Tsosie expressed great anxiety over the prospect that winter weather conditions might keep the caretaker from making regular visits. A CHR also visits Mrs. Tsosie regularly to take her blood pressure, weigh her, and check her medicine supply, and the senior center brings her a lunch each weekday. Obviously this woman is receiving the maximum benefit from the services available to the elderly, though it is significant that she lives in Tuba City, where the services are most consistently available and she is easily accessible to the service providers.

In the face of general cutbacks in IHS programs, rising transportation costs, and the focusing of IHS priorities on the provision of acute care services, the preventive health and in-home care service goals of the Community Health Representative program are threatened. In 1984, after budget cuts had eliminated three positions, there were six employees for the entire 5,000-square-mile service unit that coincided with our study area. One of the CHRs was at an entry-level position and thus was not qualified to provide direct health care to clients. Two others were assigned only to the area immediately surrounding the town of Tuba City. While this is a major center of population concentration, the three remaining CHRs were obviously severely limited in the geographical area they could effectively service. Moreover, the program is intended to serve entire communities, so the elderly are only one segment of the CHR's responsibility.

The CHR program, however, has included a specific reservation-wide focus on high-risk elderly, attempting to register them all on a community-by-community basis. Malnutrition was cited as a major problem for those of the high-risk group who have no one at home to cook for them regularly, 49 percent required assistance with hauling wood and water, and 45 percent had a chronic disease such as heart disease, kidney disease, alcoholism, diabetes, thyroid disease, seizure disorder, or high blood pressure (DHIS 1980:38). While not all high-risk elderly required home care services, others were considered to have problems severe enough to qualify them for admission to institutional care centers.

In a population in which a large proportion of the people live in locations distant from care centers, and with the push to provide community-based rather than institutional care whenever possible, CHR programs focused on training members of local communities to meet these needs. A proposal to fund a formal home health care system, integrating services from the Navajo Tribal Home Health Project, CHR (now under the auspices of the tribal department of Health Services), and CHN programs was being developed during our survey. The goal was to provide alternatives to institutional care through more coordinated in-home and community-based services. But at the same time, the CHR budget had recently been cut, and program administrators were unsure whether it would be funded at all in the next fiscal year.[7]

While tribal program objectives and health service needs point in several directions, the realities of funding cuts and eligibility restrictions create a gap between goals on the one hand and organizations capable of providing services on the other. Respondents to a survey of tribal administrators and aging-services employees raised questions concerning the extent to which Navajo tribal policies with regard to the elderly reflect the attitudes and goals of federal agencies rather than the needs and socioeconomic realities of the Navajo people (Timmreck and Brown 1984:34). But equally important are the limitations on the tribe's ability to bend federal and state policies to accommodate the changing sociocultural environment of the reservation population.

CONCLUSION

The picture of services for the elderly that emerges is that—unlike acute hospital care—it is the responsibility of everyone and no one. This is largely due to the fact that chronic care has not been recognized as a need until recently, and when it was recognized, the economic and political environment was such that the hope for obtaining generous funding for new health and social service programs was dim.[8] While this dilemma is not unique to the Navajo, it makes the task of developing culturally sensitive and ecologically appropriate programs considerably more difficult.

The current emphasis is on in-home services and family care, but this is not always a viable option. According to various tribal administrators and longtime observers of health programs on the reservation, the development of institutional facilities was prompted by the awareness that the socioeconomic changes would, in fact, result in a certain segment of the elderly population finding themselves without adequate family support and requiring constant medical attention. Attitudes toward the use of nursing homes as long-term care alternatives differed dramatically among our informants and their families. At one extreme there was strong contempt for, or fear of, the idea of being confined to such a foreign place with inedible food and being surrounded by strangers, and mostly old ones at that. When hospitals were first opened on the reservation, they were known as places to take people to die, young or old, and it is possible this perspective now is applied to nursing homes.

An alternative opinion was expressed by an elderly man who knew there would be few relatives available to care for him once his health declined. He concluded that after many decades of battling the elements, following sheep herds over wilderness terrain, and enduring the vagaries of intermittent off-reservation wage work, a clean, warm place with meals and medical care consistently available was not unappealing. In general, as long as the facility was nearby, few people we talked with rejected institutional care as a shameful way to treat their elderly relatives when there was no viable alternative.

National and eventually tribal policy priorities have shifted away from institutional care to community-based services and in-home care programs. While an overriding assumption was that such services would cost less to provide, it was also suggested that the programs could more effectively serve the general needs of most elderly. The programs are often handcuffed however, by conflicting sets of guidelines and regulations established by overlapping federal, state, and tribal administrative authorities, and their usefulness is further compromised by insufficient (at best) and erratic funding. The result is that only a limited number of the elderly, those living closest to service centers, are able to depend on them. In this context, the ideology of the family as a source of support has been especially attractive. Whether this is a reasonable approach is a question very much open to debate.

►► 8 ◄◄

EPILOGUE

WHEN WE BEGAN, we were particularly interested in determining the relationship between social isolation and measures of health status and health care utilization. Previous studies, particularly those of social support and subsequent mortality, had shown mixed results. Some showed that social support reduced the risk of death, while others showed no effect. The prevalent opinion, however, is that the association is real but that measures of social relationship or integration may be less valid or have less variance in rural areas and among women, thus muting their relationship with mortality and morbidity (House et al. 1988).

Interest in the association among social support, morbidity, and mortality originated in studies of the consequences of acculturation, social change, and modernization. The underlying assumption was generally that modernization involved a shift from extended to nuclear neolocal family organization and as a result an increased risk of social isolation. Thus, to the degree that the proportion of socially isolated people increased as a society modernized, certain morbid conditions associated with isolation would be expected to increase as well. Often these so-called diseases of civilization are thought of as the chronic noninfectious diseases that have a large psychosomatic component. Heart disease and hypertension are the conditions most often investigated in this connection.

We have found an impressive lack of association between measures of social isolation and the various measures of health. This came as a surprise because the destruction of the Navajos' pastoral economy worked immense changes in the life of the generation of elderly people who are the subjects of this study. Their career expectations were frustrated, and they lost control over their own lives. Also, changes in the size and functioning of cooperating kin networks worked considerable hardship. Certainly many of the social conditions brought about by modernization are found among the Navajo.

Part of the reason for the lack of association has to do with the fact that there is less variance in Navajo income and education, as well as the fact that no one in the study was truly isolated. In addition, many of the social indicators do not directly measure the anomie said to be produced by social isolation. That is, the quality of the social relationships is not measured, only their number and extent. The fact that survival often depends on pooling the resources of several families means that many people must live with others despite strained relationships. We did find, for example, that the frequency of depressive symptoms was higher among women who lived with impaired children. Perhaps even more important is the fact that the present generation of elderly Navajos does not suffer from the same diseases that plague the general population. To the extent that such chronic conditions as heart disease and hypertension are affected by the social environment, they may be associated with measures of social integration more than the conditions that do plague elderly Navajos.

The few positive findings of this study raise yet another issue: the degree to which very different forms of social organization may invalidate the general measures of social support used by most studies of the general population. Would the social positions of men in a matrilineal society, for example, be sufficiently different from that of men in our own society that the marriage bond or relationships with children would not have similar affective qualities? Freed and Freed (1971), for example, found that the roles of matrilineally related kin are still more important to Navajos than are those of the father's kin, and that the father's kin are less important to Navajos than they are to the bilocal and bilateral Washo Indians. These findings suggest that instead of measuring social support along a single dimension, various relationships should be measured separately and even given different weight depending on the society or subpopulation under consideration.

In some of our earlier work, we found that Navajo suicide patterns were radically different from those found in the United States in general and in Europe, where the socially isolated—the sick, aged, divorced, widowed, or single—were the most at risk for suicide. Among the Navajos the young married male was the most at risk, and rates declined after the age of 40 (Levy 1965; Levy et al. 1969). The instability of Navajo marriage and the insecure position of the younger male in his wife's matricentered kin group, we thought, accounted for this pattern. Since then, we have examined the position of men in Navajo society more closely and have suggested that the tensions characteristic of Navajo marriage were not due simply to the subordinate position of males in matrilineal society but rather to a series of changes in Navajo society since the eighteenth century that made the relationship between the sexes and the stability of the family even more conflict ridden than was the case among the Navajos' matrilineal neighbors, the Hopi and Zuni (Levy et al. 1987).

By 1700 the Navajos had come to rely on agriculture almost as much as on hunting and, influenced by their Pueblo neighbors, had become matrilineal and had often lived with Pueblos in small settlements called pueblitos. By the early 1800s, the Navajos were obtaining approximately half of their subsistence from sheep and cattle raising, an occupation that is male dominated and that created tensions between the sexes due to the fact that women already occupied a central role in the domestic economy. Then, as the population grew and dispersed across an ever-expanding reservation in the nineteenth century, family isolation exacerbated tensions. Men worked their wives' herds but would leave their own at home in the care of their mothers and sisters. The social bonds that appear to have been the most enduring and supportive prior to stock reduction were those between mothers and daughters, and among sisters. Brother-sister and husband-wife bonds were more ambivalent, although by the time old age was reached, the intensity of marital tensions may have lessened.

When viewed in this context, the few associations we found between measures of social support and health status have some significance. Hypertension was the measure of health status that was associated with measures of both acculturation and social isolation. Women had an increased risk of hypertension the more acculturated and isolated they were. For men, however, measures of involvement in the larger society were associated with decreased risk of hypertension. We interpret this to mean that isolation and involvement in the wage economy weakened the supportive mother-daughter and sister-sister bonds but allowed men some escape from traditional social constraints while permitting them to attain more economic autonomy.

Other positive findings were more ambiguous. Although the symptoms of depression were sensitive to measures of social support, diagnosed depression was not. Women who lived with their daughters tended to be less at risk for depression, and all the women who had never raised daughters were depressed. But preexisting personality problems accounted for the fact that some women neither bore children nor were given children to raise by their sisters, and depression itself seems to account for a large proportion of the women who were alienated from their daughters.

Unmarried men living without children or in isolation had higher mortality if they were 75 or older. But some of these men also had long histories of heavy drinking so that both social isolation and death may well have been the consequence of alcohol abuse. Drinking may, in fact, be a key to understanding male health patterns and social relationships. If the picture we have drawn of the male's position in Navajo society is correct—that many of them have few, if any, supportive relationships they can rely on—we would expect depression to be more prevalent among them. If, however, drinking has come to be the expression of Navajo male anomie, it would explain a number of findings. Those few men we were able to diagnose as depressed (because they were married and their wives gave the information) all drank, and it seems likely that drinking masks depression, which may be far more prevalent among males than we were able to determine. The degree to which alcohol abuse obscures correlations with measures of social integration and support, and the degree to which it may of itself affect male health status must be studied in more detail.

We have said that one reason for the lack of strong associations between social isolation and measures of health status may be that the prevalent patterns of morbidity and mortality in this cohort are unrelated to measures of social isolation. Elderly Navajos have lower age-specific death rates from all causes, especially cancer and heart disease, and lower rates of hospitalization than are observed in the general U.S. population. On the other hand, the general level of function seems not to be significantly different from what is observed among non-Indians. Level of function is a different way of measuring morbidity from the diagnosis of a specific disease condition, and it may be unrelated to measures of social integration and support. In our sample—and presumably in other populations as well—function seems to reflect two separable phenomena: the wear and tear of growing old in a rigorous environment and diagnosable, often life-threatening diseases. High levels of dysfunction among men below age 75 reflected primarily life-threatening conditions. High levels among people 75 and older are as likely to reflect conditions that cause disability but that may not be life-threatening.

This raises a serious policy issue, for it is diagnosable conditions that are widely agreed to be health problems. The problems of "normal" dysfunction are less widely agreed to be health problems and, depending on prevailing policies, may or may not attract attention from care providers. The very real improvement in the health of Navajos over the past forty years is to a large degree a result of the preventive and curative services provided by the Indian Health Services (Kunitz 1983). But the skills and institutional infrastructure that have been so effective in reducing deaths from the pneumonia-diarrhea complex of childhood and from tuberculosis are not well suited to providing the kinds of supportive services required by people whose problems are largely the consequence of normal aging in a rigorous environment. The policy of paying for skilled but not custodial or home care exemplifies the problem. Further, it is not uniquely a Navajo problem but is instead confronted by many elderly people in our society. Implicit in government policy at the federal, state, and local levels is the idea that if dysfunction is not the result of such a disease entity, then care should only be provided after the individual and his or her family have been pauperized.

This policy is of a piece with the way health insurance has evolved during this century. Since the 1930s, insurance has gone from simply making up for income lost as a result of illness to paying medical costs (Starr 1982). But this creates a difficult problem, for as Starr (1982:290) has pointed out, "Insurance ordinarily requires that any hazard insured against and the losses arising from it be unambiguous when they occur and beyond the control of the insured." This is the problem of "moral hazard": that the presence of insurance should not increase the risk of the event being insured against. The Indian Health Service is not an insurance program, but the principle is broadly the same: the availability of care may encourage people to redefine their functional abilities in such a fashion as to place excessive demands on existing services. That is to say, without the clarity of a diagnosis, costs may escalate and become unpredictable and "abuse" of the system may occur. While it is understandable why such clarity is required, it has meant that attention is necessarily focused on episodes of illness rather than on the level of function and such ambiguous questions as degree of mobility and loss of independence.

We would argue, however, that such an essentialist conception of health problems is too confining. The conditions with which elderly people must cope cannot so easily be identified as the result of either disease or normal aging. We take a more nominalist position regarding the definition of a health problem. While not as extreme as Humpty Dumpty, who claimed that words meant exactly what he chose them to mean, neither more nor less, we think that definitions of health (and other) problems are largely the result of debate and negotiation among interested groups, both lay and professional (Blumer 1971). Moreover, precisely because the IHS is not an insurance-based program, it is ideally situated to provide care to elderly people whose functional abilities are waning. Insurance provides protection from risk, not certainty. Declining levels of function with increasing age fall in the latter category, not the former. While "abuse" of the system is, of course, always a possibility, abuse by a system that is unable or unwilling to adapt to a changing epidemiologic and demographic regime is closer to being a reality.

Although these observations are applicable to non-Indians as well as Indians, the latter are of particular concern, for two reasons. Not only do many elderly Indians experience diminished function, but the conventional wisdom suggests that extended families are available to provide the needed help. It is true that miltihousehold camps as well as multigeneration households still exist and continue to be adaptive to the current economic situation, thus accounting for the very small number of extreme isolates in our sample. But large kin networks capable of mustering manpower for a wide variety of purposes, including caring for disabled elderly people, no longer exist.

The increasing difficulties faced by once-wealthy families who can no longer support their elderly members as they once did is not a reflection of the devastating effects of dependence on welfare or the professional imperialism of service providers, as has sometimes been suggested. It is the result of the destruction of the livestock economy and the failure to replace it with a viable, productive alternative. Dependence on unearned income has been the result of that failure, and if the formerly wealthy are no longer able to manage as they once did, then those who have always been poor have presumably had an even more difficult time of it.

Thus, to invoke the family as the source of support seems at best naive and at worst pernicious. The level of support required by many elderly people cannot be provided by kin. What makes the current situation at all manageable is the still low proportion of elderly people in the population and the thus-far low rates of disability from such chronic diseases as diabetes.

Neither situation will last. A declining birth rate as well as emigration are sure to result in an increasing proportion of elderly in the population. Further, the increasing incidence of diabetes seems certain to lead to many sequelae that the Navajos to date have been largely spared: chronic renal failure, diabetic retinopathy, and gangrenous limbs, to name just a few. All of this will require supportive—even custodial—services the likes of which the IHS and the BIA have not yet had to provide on a truly major scale. It is not too early to start planning for the time when such problems will have overwhelmed whatever capacities families still have to provide support to their elderly dependent members.

How does what we have observed of the health and social conditions of our informants speak to concerns about aging more generally? The notion of "triple jeopardy" has been suggested to describe the situation of people who are old, poor, and members of a minority group. Being old means to be increasingly infirm, being poor means to be unable to purchase needed goods and services, and being a member of a minority group means that the institutions of the larger society are not likely to be designed to suit one's culturally specific needs.

"Triple jeopardy" is not an adequate description of the situation of the elderly of every ethnic minority, nor is it an entirely adequate label for the situation of the people with whom we worked. Infirm many of them undoubtedly were, but no more so (and no less so) than non-Indians. That they were poor and unable to command adequate purchasing power is undoubtedly true. On the other hand, being an elderly Navajo living on the Navajo Reservation is not like being an elderly black or Hispanic person in an American city. First, on the Navajo Reservation elderly Navajos are not members of a minority group. Second, because of the unique relationship between some Indian tribes and the federal government, there is a greater potential that formal institutions will be responsive to the special needs of this particular group of elderly citizens. As we have suggested, such a relationship does not guarantee responsiveness: it simply makes it more likely.

To the degree that social and economic changes have reduced the ability of kinsmen to care for elderly sick members, however, the situation of the Navajos is clearly similar to that of many other peoples, be they members of minority groups or of the majority. For all these people, formal institutions that provide care and support are assuming a growing role, even as family and friends continue to contribute in a wide variety of ways. As we have said, because increasing disability with age is closer to being a certainty than a risk, insurance is not the way to support such services. Widely accessible care paid for out of general revenues would seem to be more appropriate. The Indian Health Service is unique in the United States as just such an organization. It thus stands as a potential model of how such services could be provided for the elderly in general. As yet, however, that potential has not been realized.

►► Appendix 1 ◄◄

SAMPLING TECHNIQUES

OUR SAMPLE WAS CHOSEN from a computer-generated list of all people who had been seen in one of the hospitals or field clinics in the Tuba City Service Unit during the ten-year period 1972–1981, who had been born before 1917 (that is, who were 65 or older in 1982 when the field-work began), and who gave an address within the Tuba City Service Unit. A great deal of time was spent eliminating those entries that (1) were under the age of 65, (2) had home communities that were outside the service unit boundaries, or (3) had multiple entries for the same individual, who may have been seen several times during the decade or who may have utilized two or even three of the available health facilities.

Once these eliminations had been made, there were 1,660 entries, many more than the 500 to 600 that the 1980 census had led us to expect. The entries were transferred to 3 × 5 cards, each numbered sequentially and containing the individual's hospital unit number, date of birth, and community (or communities) of residence. The cards were then taken to the medical records section of the Tuba City hospital and checked against a concordance linking unit numbers and individual names. No medical charts were reviewed at this time. At a later date, after obtaining informed consent, Kunitz reviewed the medical charts, which listed the ICD9 codes for morbidities experienced by each individual.

A sample of 880 individuals was then selected from the original

1,660 cards by using a random-number generater with an upper limit of 1,660. The sample was then checked against two permanent files in the medical records section, an IHS unit number–date of birth concordance, and an IHS unit number–mortality file. This review eliminated a number of individuals whose birth dates had been incorrectly entered into the computer listing of patients seen as well as a number of individuals who had died. Field interviewing further eliminated several individuals who were not permanent residents of the Tuba City Service Unit. The final sample consisted of 278 individuals, of whom we were able to contact and interview 270.

Navajo Population, a publication of the Office of Program Planning and Statistics (U.S. Public Health Service 1980), estimated that the total service-unit population was 12,779 in 1980. Of these, 542 (4.2 percent) were over the age of 65. The 1980 census estimated the portion of the Navajo Reservation within Conconino County (which also includes about 46 percent of the Bird Springs, Leupp, and Tolani Lake chapters of the Winslow Service Unit) contained 15,306 individuals, of whom 612 (4 percent) were 65 or older. The Indian Health Service estimate for the same area and year (1980) was 18,201. The latter estimate differs by about 16 percent of the total population and 20 percent of the population over 65 years of age. It was based on the U.S. census of 1970 with annual adjustments based on estimates of births, deaths, and in- and out-migration by county.

The IHS estimate would lead us to anticipate about 764 individuals over 65. The 1980 Census, which has a history of underreporting Native Americans, actually enumerated 612 individuals. We believe that the census underreported and that the IHS adjustments overestimated. For our purposes it seemed reasonable to estimate that about 4.1 percent of the Navajo population in this area is 65 years of age or over. Using this proportion and adjusting the IHS projections for 1983, which are the best available, we would expect about 578 individuals in this age cohort to be living in the Tuba City Service Unit in 1983, the year most of the interviews were conducted. The 270 individuals finally interviewed represented about 47 percent of the estimated total population.

The fundamental reason for interviewing such a large proportion of the target population was the complexity of the research topic. Not only did important variables, such as camp organization, contain a number of mutually exclusive attributes but certain age-linked morbidities—organic brain syndrome, for example—had low prevalence.

In the case of camp organization, which was one of the most important measures of social support, no intuitive taxonomy of social relations was apparent prior to the beginning of the study. Indeed, previous work on this topic in the same locale had indicated that camp organization was a complex and heterogeneous phenomenon.

After the interviews were completed, more than 150 mutually exclusive "types" of camps were identified, which might indicate variations in social support. In fact, so varied was the descriptive approach to this phenomenon that we were forced to adopt a "structural" typology focusing on four dimensions: (1) single individuals versus conjugal pairs in the apical generation; (2) the generational depth of the camp (1 to 4 generations); (3) the nature of social linkages (primary, secondary, or both); (4) the presence or absence of transient residents in the camp.

In terms of health planning and the estimation of future demands for services, certain age-related morbidities are devastating and extremely expensive to treat. They occur, however, in only a small proportion of the population. For such morbidities to be adequately represented, the sample had to be sufficiently large to insure their inclusion.

We thus anticipated that much of the most important information would be heterogeneous. To avoid empty or low-frequency cells in bivariate and multivariate analysis of mixed (nominal, ordinal, and interval) data sets, the proportion of the target population had to be large. For example, one runs out of cases very rapidly when attempting to differentiate or associate the independent effects of household or camp organization, income, and religious participation on a specific morbidity. Attempting to parcel out the effects of even two nominal heterogeneous variables can easily create a number of empty cells.

We also anticipated that this study might form the basis for prospective study of morbidity and mortality. Given the risk of mortality in this elderly age group, a sufficiently large sample had to be selected to allow for attrition during the next decade. It is arguable that the selected sample of 270 was large enough for our purposes; in such circumstances large numbers are always preferable. Resources and logistics were the important limiting factors. Contacting 270 individuals randomly distributed in an area the size of the state of Rhode Island with only three paved roads, virtually no telephones, and no "addresses" is an extremely difficult and time-consuming process. Identifying and contacting individuals (many were assigned two or three Anglo names by different bureaucrats); locating their current community of residence, often from a list of four or five possibilities; and driving two or three hours, with frequent stops to confirm directions on unpaved roads with only the most general landmarks, only to find the individual away from home or moved to a sheep camp is a frustrating experience. Various strategies were devised to help minimize these logistical difficulties. Community Health Representatives were a great help in identifying and locating people, and interviewers always left for distant communities with three or four possible interviewees as alternative contacts for the return trip.

Despite these efforts, it was not unusual for an interview—including verification of the person, arranging for an appointment, and the interview itself—to take three days to complete. Those familiar with the extremely rural character of the Navajo Reservation are aware of the difficulties imposed by bad weather and rugged terrain on survey research.

Enlarging the area to include communities outside the Tuba City Service Unit would have yielded diminished returns. Even so, being centrally located in Tuba City still required a full day in round-trip travel for many interviews. This restriction had the unfortunate consequence of eliminating those individuals who utilized the Tuba City hospital but who lived outside the service unit. Given the waiting time in clinics and the travel time involved, many people would spend the night with relatives prior to their return home. In consequence, this sample is representative of the service unit but may neglect a residual population that forms a portion of the total demand for medical services. This residual population is not biased in any way we can ascertain, however, and probably consists of less than 20 percent of the total demand for service at the Tuba City hospital.

A simple calculation indicates that, given the target population of 578 individuals, and a 47 percent random sample of 271, we can be 95 percent confident that our estimates of various pathologies and the like are within 6 percent of the true population proportions.

In some respects, the questions asked were contradictory in their sampling demands. The need to make representative statements about the distribution of disease and disability in the population required that a large proportion of the total be randomly sampled. On the other hand, the nature of "social support" implies interdependent rather than independent social relationships. The analysis of social support might better have been served by a "network approach," in which units of analysis are neither randomly sampled nor, in the statistical sense, considered to be independent but where links of social support are followed as they radiate from an individual. In this "snowball" process an individual defines his or her major supporters and these individuals are then contacted and interviewed to discover their perception of the support they provide. Such a technique might have provided a more complete picture of the total support system. Such an approach, however, would have severely limited the size of the study population, since resources would have been used to interview supporting individuals, the majority of whom would have been under the age of 65 and nonrandomly selected.

It seemed more important to be confident about the representativeness of the sample and to have enough cases to make reasonable inferences about the relationships from the data in hand than to trace the complete context of social support. Naturally, a number of questions were included in the interview to determine who provided support to the informants and the nature of that support. This decision precluded any chance of gaining an intimate understanding of support networks.

➤ Appendix 2 ◄

THE NAVAJO AGING PROJECT QUESTIONNAIRE

WE ARE DOING a survey of problems of elderly people living on the Navajo Reservation. We would appreciate it if you would answer some questions for us about your health and how you are getting along. After the interview is completed, we will pay you ten dollars. The information you give us will be strictly confidential. The results of the study will be made available to the Indian Health Service, the Navajo Tribe, and the Bureau of Indian Affairs in order to help them plan better health services for elderly Navajos.

1. CAMP NUMBER _____

2. INFORMANT NUMBER _____

3. Community of residence _____

4. Distance from paved road (in miles) _____

5. Distance from nearest hospital _____

6. Distance from nearest clinic _____

7. Name of clinic _____

8. How long have you lived in this camp? _____

9. In this community? _____

10. If resident in Tuba City, what were the reasons for moving there? _____

11. If resident outside of Tuba City, are there any circumstances under which it might be necessary to move there? If so, what are they? _____

12. Number and type of dwellings in camp (Check each that applies):

	0	1	2	3	4
Hogan(s)					
House(s)					
Trailer(s)					

13. Facilities available (check each that applies):

	None	In Camp	In Respondent's Dwelling
Running water			
Indoor toilet			
Electricity			

14. Number of rooms in respondent's dwelling _____

15. Respondent's type of dwelling (circle one):   hogan   house   trailer

16. How many different places have you lived for more than 2 weeks in the past 3 months? _____

MAP OF CAMP

17. Camp composition

Dwelling no.	Name	Relation- ship to informant	Sex	Age	Education Status p = perm t = temp aw = away	Occupa- tion	Place of birth	Comment

18. WAGE WORK

Name of indiv.	Employer	No. of months worked in past 24 mos.	Position	Approximate annual salary

19. UNEARNED INCOME (List amount under each source)

Name of indiv.	Soc. sec.	Pension	ADC	Unemployment	Tribal welfare	Other

20. Does the camp receive food stamps? (circle one)   Yes   No   Unknown

21. Does the camp receive surplus commodities?   Yes   No   Unknown

22. Number of sheep owned by camp: _____

23. Number of cattle owned by camp: _____

24. Does informant own a stock permit?   Yes   No

25. If so, for how many head? _____

26. If informant does not own one, did he/she ever own one?   Yes   No   Unknown

27. If he/she did once own one, why did he/she get rid of it? _____

28. When did he/she get rid of it? _____

29. To whom was permit given? _____

30. Number of pickups or sedans in camp (that work): _____

SUPPORT NETWORKS

31. Who usually gives you a ride when you need to buy things or go to the hospital or clinic? (Note: if person named is not a relative, ask how the informant knows him or her; e.g., member of same church.)

Name of individual	Relationship to informant	How distant	Pay for gas/ride?

32. If you are sick, who comes to take care of you?

Name of individual	Relationship to informant	Where does he/she live?

33. Have you had a Sing within the past year?　　　　Yes　　No　　Unknown

34. How many days did it last? _____

35. When was the last time you had a Sing? _____

36. The last time you had a Sing, who were the major contributors?

Name	Relationship to informant	Residence	Nature and extent of aid

37. Who outside of the camp helps in shearing, dipping, herding, and/or transporting sheep?

Name	Relationship to informant	Residence	Frequency	Charge?

38. Who outside the camp aids in hauling of wood and water?

Name	Relationship to informant	Residence	Frequency	Charge?

39. Who outside the camp comes to visit most frequently?

Name	Relationship to informant	Residence	Frequency of visits

40. Who do you regularly visit outside of this camp?

Name	Relationship to informant	Residence	Frequency of visits

ACTIVITIES

41. What are the major activities you do during the week? For example:
42. Participate in Home Care program? _____
43. If yes, due to what illness? _____
44. Visited by CHR? _____
45. If yes, for what reason? _____
46. Attend senior citizens' groups? _____ How often? _____ Why? _____
47. Herd sheep? _____
48. Do weaving or beadwork? _____
49. Attend Chapter meetings?   Rarely   Occasionally   Frequently
50. Attend Church?   Rarely   Occasionally   Frequently
51. If so, which one (e.g., NAC, Christian)? _____
52. What kinds of activities do you most look forward to during the week? _____

SICKNESS IMPACT PROFILE: AMBULATION

	Check here for affirmative answer	(Score for affirmative answer)	Check here if question was answered by proxy
53. I walk shorter distances or stop to rest often.		048	
54. I do not walk up or down hills.		056	
55. I walk up hills only with mechanical support, for example, cane, crutches.		067	
56. I walk up or down hills only with assistance from someone else.		076	
57. I get around in a wheelchair.		096	
58. I do not walk at all.		105	
59. I walk by myself but with some difficulty; for example, limp, wobble, stumble, have stiff leg.		055	
60. I walk only with help from someone.		088	
61. I go up and down hills more slowly; for example, one step at a time, stop often.		054	
62. I get around only using a walker, crutches, cane, walls, or furniture.		079	
63. I walk more slowly.		035	
64. I get around as easily as ever.	Yes	No	Unknown

SICKNESS IMPACT PROFILE: MOBILITY

	Check here for affirmative answer	(Score for affirmative answer)	Check here if question was answered by proxy
65. I get around only within my house (or hogan or trailer).		086	
66. I am staying in bed more.		081	
67. I am staying in bed most of the time.		109	
68. I stay at home most of the time.		066	
69. I do not go to the trading post.		048	
70. I stay away from home only for brief periods of time.		054	
71. I do not get around in the dark or in unlit places without someone's help.		072	

SICKNESS IMPACT PROFILE: BODY CARE AND MOVEMENT

	Yes	Occas.	No	(Score for affirmative answer)	Check here if question was answered by proxy
72. I make difficult moves with help; for example, getting into or out of cars or pickups.				084	
73. I do not move into or out of bed or chair by myself but am moved by a person or mechanical aid.				121	
74. I stand only for short periods of time.				072	
75. I do not maintain balance.				098	
76. I move my hands or fingers with some limitation or difficulty.				064	
77. I stand up only with someone's help.				100	
78. I kneel, stoop, or bend down only by holding on to something.				064	
79. I am in a restricted position all the time.				125	
80. I am very clumsy in body movements.				058	
81. I get in and out of bed or chairs by grasping something for support or using a cane or walker.				082	
82. I stay lying down most of the time.				113	
83. I change position frequently.				030	
84. I hold on to something to move myself around in bed.				086	
85. I do not bathe myself completely; for example, require assistance with bathing.				089	
86. I do not bathe myself at all but am bathed by someone else.				115	
87. I use a bedpan with assistance.				114	
88. I have trouble getting on shoes, socks, or stockings.				057	
89. I do not have control of my bladder.				124	
90. I do not fasten my clothing; for example, require help with buttons, zippers, shoelaces.				074	
91. I spend most of the time partly undressed or in pajamas.				074	
92. I do not have control of my bowels.				128	
93. I dress myself but do so very slowly.				043	
94. I get dressed only with someone's help.				088	

SICKNESS IMPACT PROFILE: SOCIAL INTERACTION

	Check here for affirmative answer	(Score for affirmative answer)	Check here if question was answered by proxy
95. I am going out less to visit people.	————	044	————
96. I am not going out to visit people at all.	————	101	————
97. I show less interest in other people's problems; for example, don't listen when they tell me about their problems, don't offer help.	————	067	————
98. I often act irritable toward those around me; for example, snap at people, give sharp answers, criticize easily.	————	084	————
99. I show less affection.	————	052	————
100. I am doing fewer social activities with groups of people.	————	036	————
101. I am cutting down the length of visits with friends.	————	043	————
102. I am avoiding social visits from others.	————	080	————
103. I often express concern over what might be happening to my health.	————	052	————
104. I talk less with those around me.	————	056	————
105. I make many demands; for example, insist that people do things for me, tell them how to do things.	————	088	————
106. I stay alone much of the time.	————	086	————
107. I act disagreeably to family members; for example, I am spiteful, am stubborn.	————	088	————
108. I have frequent outbursts of anger at family members; for example, strike at them, scream, throw things at them.	————	119	————
109. I isolate myself as much as I can from the rest of the family.	————	102	————
110. I am paying less attention to the children.	————	064	————
111. I refuse contact with family members; for example, turn away from them.	————	115	————
112. I am not doing the things I usually do to take care of my children or family.	————	079	————
113. I am not joking with family members as I usually do.	————	043	————

SICKNESS IMPACT PROFILE: ALERTNESS BEHAVIOR

	Check here for affirmative answer	(Score for affirmative answer)	Check here if question was answered by proxy
114. I am confused and start several actions at a time.	_____	090	_____
115. I have minor accidents; for example, drop things, trip and fall, bump into things.	_____	075	_____
116. I react slowly to things that are said or done.	_____	059	_____
117. I do not finish things I start.	_____	067	_____
118. I have difficulty making plans, making decisions, learning new things.	_____	084	_____
119. I sometimes behave as if I were confused or disoriented in place or time; for example, where I am, who is around, directions, what day it is.	_____	113	_____
120. I forget a lot; for example, things that happened recently, where I put things, appointments.	_____	078	_____
121. I do not keep my attention on any activity for long.	_____	067	_____
122. I make more mistakes than usual.	_____	064	_____
123. I have difficulty doing activities involving concentration and thinking.	_____	080	_____

DEPRESSION BEHAVIORS

(If the answer to any of these items is *yes,* ask the supplemental questions at the end of the scale. Remind informant that these questions refer to the present and the past couple of years.)

124. Have you had periods of at least 2 weeks during which you felt depressed and did not care about anything anymore?	Yes	No
125. Have there been times when you felt you were not a good person, that you were useless and a burden to others?	Yes	No
126. Was there a time when you did not want to eat?	Yes	No
127. Did you ever lose a lot of weight when you were not trying to?	Yes	No
128. Have there been times when you had trouble going to sleep, staying asleep, or waking too easily?	Yes	No
129. Have there been times when you felt tired all the time?	Yes	No
130. Have there been times when you had to be moving all the time—that is, you couldn't keep still and had to get up and walk?	Yes	No
131. Has there been a time when you felt that life was not worth living and that you wanted to die?	Yes	No
132. Have you ever thought of killing yourself?	Yes	No
133. Have you ever tried to kill yourself?	Yes	No

For each of the preceding questions relating to depression where an affirmative answer is given, ask the following questions:

134. Duration of episode. _____

135. When it happened. _____

136. Surrounding circumstances; for example, associated with an illness, loss of loved one, etc. _____

137. Whether there is a history of similar episodes and, if so, when did they start. _____

138. Were any of the depression questions answered by anyone other than the elderly informant?   Yes   No

139. If yes, who was it? _____

140. Which questions? _____   _____

AUTOBIOGRAPHY

141. Were you ever in the military service? _____

142. Have you ever lived off the reservation? _____

143. If so, for how many years? _____

144. What years? _____

145. What kind of work did you do (off-reservation)? _____

146. Did you work all year long? _____

147. Did your wife and children live with you when you worked off-reservation? _____

148. Have you learned any Navajo Sings (ceremonies or parts of ceremonies) or long prayers? _____

149. Any herbal medicines? _____

150. Hand trembling? _____

151. If so, are you still practicing? _____

152. Have you ever held a chapter office? _____

153. If so, where? _____

154. And when? _____

CONSENT FORM

I hereby give consent for the staff of the *Navajo Aging Project* to review my medical records at the Tuba City hospital and health stations. I understand that the information will remain confidential.

Shi k'ad naabeehó hadást'íhí'gii yindaalnishigii bích'į' lá'asélįį, áko binįįyehigii éí tóaneesdizigi azee'al'indóó shínaaltsoos beeshééhozhinigii dáadinoołʼiił. Ako she bik'idiitáago t'eiya naaltsoos beeshééhozhinigii t'ááiiyisii naaniiłʼíndoo biniiyé.

_____	_____
Date	Signed

_____	_____
Tuba City Indian Hospital Unit Number	Witness

Notes

2 The Changing Contexts of Aging

1. This includes cattle, each equivalent to four sheep, but does not include horses, which were not sold or consumed.

3 Social Organization, Morbidity, and Hospital Use

1. The scales we used are reproduced in Appendix 2. As the interviews were lengthy, we could not use all the scales included in the original instrument (Dept. of Health Services, University of Washington 1977). Moreover, a few of the original questions in the scales we did use were inappropriate in the Navajo context and were dropped. Others had to be reworded (e.g., climbing stairs was changed to climbing hills). The scales have been scored in a number of ways in other studies (Gilson et al. 1975). We chose the simplest, summing the scores assigned by the developers of the scales (Bergner et al. 1976a and 1976b; Pollard et al. 1976). We also scored them on an ordinal three-point scale: yes, sometimes, and no. The results were so highly correlated with the assigned interval scores that only the latter are used throughout.

2. A Kruskall-Wallis analysis of variance yielded significant differences among both means and medians among men and women grouped by age: under 75 and 75 and above. The most significant differences (p = .0001) were in the PHYSIP and TOTSIP, the least significant (p = .04) in the SOISIP.

3. Pearson's correlations gave p values between .05 and .0001 for both men and women. Rank order correlations gave essentially identical results.

4. We made no distinction among tests with regard to complexity or cost.

A barium enema and a blood count were given the same weight. The Public Health Service does not charge for tests or other services unless the patient has third-party coverage. There was, in consequence, no uniform and readily available way to review bills and use dollar amounts as a measure of the intensity of use. Moreover, since some of the patients were treated in other facilities and only discharge summaries were available, there was an inevitable undercounting of diagnostic tests. Because outpatient services are obtained in a wide variety of clinics in the region, the visits made to the Tuba City Hospital outpatient department were not included in the present analysis.

5. Under 75: 7 over 40 days, 32 under 40 days. Over 75: 1 over 40 days, 48 under 40 days ($\chi^2 = 4.86$; df = 1; $p < .05$).

6. Rough calculations assuming (a) that there was 3 percent ECF utilization in Massachusetts (comparable to what we have estimated for the Navajos), and (b) that the Massachusetts people in our estimate who were then no longer institutionalized were all dependent in dressing and transfer did not alter the result significantly. The reason for making this adjustment is that very disabled people in Massachusetts may be removed to extended care facilities, whereas Navajos tend to remain at home. Thus the comparison might be biased in such a way as to make Massachusetts respondents living in the community appear to have better function than the entire surviving cohort actually does.

7. We performed a logistic regression: hospital use (yes or no) adjusted for age, sex, and marital status.

8. The number of individuals was, unfortunately, very small in some of the categories. Nonetheless, when the measures of hospital use were compared by two-way analyses of variance, with age-sex and marital status as the independent variables, no significant differences were revealed.

9. Because these are camps in which elderly people live, they are not necessarily representative of the distribution of all camps. For example, in Red Lake in the 1970s, 61 percent of all camps were neolocal, compared to only 43 percent of camps in which elderly people lived in this study.

10. We did a series of analyses of covariance for men and women separately. The independent variables were camp type and age of respondent, and the SIP scales were the dependent variables. Not surprisingly, age had an effect.

11. We did a logistical regression for each of the measures of camp size. PHYSIP, age, sex, and camp size were the independent variables, and whether hospitalized or not was the dependent variable. In both instances, only PHYSIP was significantly related to hospitalization. Identical results were obtained when number of children in camp was substituted for camp size.

12. It is not clear why there should be an inverse relationship between camp size and PHYSIP among hospitalized men below the age of 75. It persisted when the men with extreme PHYSIP scores were removed from the analysis. There was no association between years in camp and either hospital days or PHYSIP, indicating that the most disabled men do not move to large camps

as a result of their disability and ill health. Also, there was no relationship between PHYSIP and camp size in the entire sample of men, including all who were not hospitalized as well as those who were. We believe this is most likely a fortuitous association, the result of having done so many statistical tests.

13. Pearson's and Spearman's correlations were done for each age-sex group by PHYSIP, ALBSIP, and SOISIP.

14. Type of camp (independent neolocal = 1; extended = 2); number of permanent residents in camp (single person = 0; two or more = 1); presence of respondent's children in camp (not present = 0; present = 4); frequent visiting of respondent's children from within a five-mile radius (no visiting or little visiting = 0; frequent visiting = 3); and marital status (not married = 0; married = 5).

15. The difference was significant (χ^2 = 26.307; df = 2; p = .001). There were 63 men with high social integration scores, 46 with medium, and 15 with low scores. Among women there were 31 with high, 93 with medium, and 21 with low scores.

16. Because neither the social isolation measure nor days in hospital is normally distributed, we collapsed the former into low, medium, and high categories and then used the Kruskall-Wallis one-way analysis of variance to compare the rank order of days among categories, treating men and women separately. For neither sex were the results significant.

17. The controls were chosen by listing for each person with an impaired offspring all the people of the same age and sex, numbering them and then selecting one using a random-number generator. The matched pairs were then compared using the Wilcoxon signed-ranks test.

18. Only ceremonialists and 8 controls had been hospitalized at least once during the study period, too small a number to reach statistical significance. Together, the 24 ceremonialists averaged 6.4 days in hospital, compared to 8 days for the controls.

6 MORTALITY

1. In 1910 there were 903 people aged 65 and over out of a total population of 23,377. By 1978 these numbers had increased to 4,553 out of a tribal population of 129,868 (Johnston 1966:156–166; U.S. Department of the Interior 1972; Carr 1978; Navajo Tribe 1978; U.S. Bureau of the Census 1982).

2. The estimated range of mortality rates for 1972–78 was calculated in the following way: The numerator was deaths in 1972–78 of all Indians 65 and above giving a reservation address (see Kunitz 1983 for details). Since the denominator (all Navajos 65 and above living on-reservation) was not accurately known, we took high and low estimates. The Navajo Tribe's Department on Aging estimated the 1975 population to have been 4,242 (Carr 1978). Another tribal estimate, for 1978, was 6,025 people 65 and above (Navajo Tribe 1978). We have taken 6,000 as the upper boundary of the 1975 population. This

upper limit may not be too far off the mark. The lower limit is almost certainly too low. The number of Navajos 65 and above enumerated on-reservation in the 1980 census was 6,354. Based upon our sampling in Districts 1 and 3, we believe the census may have undernumerated the elderly population by as much as 15 percent. Nonetheless, for our purposes the range we have selected is adequate.

3. Using the usual chi-square test, the differences between the married and unmarried did not attain the conventional level of significance (chi-square = 3.03; $p > .05$). Fisher's Exact Test, however, yielded significant results ($p < .05$).

4. Ninety percent confidence limits are used to conform with the one-tailed test.

5. These groups were combined to increase numbers for the analysis.

7 Perspectives on Caring for the Elderly

1. The term New Federalism is used in a bill introduced to the U.S. Senate entitled "New Federalism for American Indians Act of 1990." It describes the congressional goal of "provid[ing] each tribe with an annual grant equal to its proportional share of the current Federal Indian budget, as a permanent entitlement with a cost-of-living allowance, in lieu of Federal programs and services." Tribes would enter into New Federalism Agreements with the federal government on a voluntary basis. The bill was under consideration during the summer of 1990.

2. In 1988, efforts were initiated to create an Office of Native American Programs within the Administration on Aging, which would administer and oversee services to Indian elders. The legislative mandate for the new office is included in the Older Americans Act Amendments of 1987 (PL 100-175), signed into law in late November.

3. The Arizona Long Term Care System (ALTCS) began in January 1989 under AHCCCS and serves the elderly, physically disabled, and developmentally disabled. As of August 1990, about 7 percent of its participants were American Indian. Also, in a move unprecedented in Arizona's history, a state-level Advisory Council on Indian Health Care was appointed at the close of 1989. It is responsible for assessing the health care needs of American Indians in Arizona, and it includes representatives from twenty tribes.

4. On October 5, 1988, the Indian Self-Determination Act Amendments (PL 100-472) were signed into law in response to the difficulties inherent in the tribal contracting and program management processes established under the original act. The goal of the amendments is to stabilize funding for tribal contracts and to increase tribal participation in the management of federal Indian programs. A specific policy change addressed by PL 100-472 is that tribal indirect costs for program management, which were excluded from contracts under the provisions of the original act, will now be covered. It is too soon to assess the actual impact of the amendments, and while the intentions seem laudable in print, there are many potential obstacles to attaining

the act's goals. For example, if Congress does not increase funding for IHS and BIA programs overall to levels that can absorb the additional 17 percent for tribal indirect program costs, there will essentially be a reduction in monies available for tribally run programs.

5. In March 1990, Rosalyn Curtis became the first woman candidate for president in the Navajo tribal primary elections. She noted a number of important issues not being recognized by the current administration or the other candidates in the running at that time. For example, Curtis reportedly supports using more tribal funds to build nursing homes on the reservation and suggested "more workers to visit and assist those elderly who want to remain at home" (*Navajo Times* [Window Rock, Ariz], March 22, 1990).

6. In August 1990 Toyei became the first Indian-owned nursing home in Arizona's history to receive long term care funds through AHCCCS, the state's alternative Medicaid program. Funds will pay for services to residents who are members of the recently initiated Arizona Long Term Care System, which is run by AHCCCS. Officials of the AHCCCS program ruled that the nursing home's request for payment of services through the ALTCS was valid because the BIA, formerly the sole funding source for Toyei, is stipulated by federal statutes as "payer of last resort." AHCCCS therefore becomes first payer, and in 1990 almost 40 percent of Toyei's residents were ALTCS members. These funds can be used to pay for both direct services to patients and badly needed equipment and repairs to the facility. Such changes will not only improve patient care but will also help qualify the facility for other sources of funding (*Navajo Times*, August 9, 1990).

7. After a six-year battle, the Indian Health Care Amendments of 1988 (PL 100-713; November 23, 1988) were signed into law. They reauthorized the original act, which expired in 1984. The amendments specifically define IHS responsibility for several health promotion efforts outside of reservation-based hospital and clinic settings that had been targeted for elimination, including the Community Health Representatives (now termed Community Health Workers within the Navajo tribal Community Health Services program). Whether this legislative mandate will be met with a federal appropriation of funds through the IHS sufficient to support the Community Health Workers program effectively remains to be seen.

8. IHS has recently begun to emphasize a change in its health care priorities such that delivery of acute care does not overshadow health promotion and disease prevention programs. In 1989 the IHS defined in the following order the areas of emphasis for research: (1) chronic disease, (2) individual responsibility for health, (3) dysfunctional families, (4) alcoholism, drug abuse and mental health problems, (5) health and health care of the elderly, (6) research in nursing, and (7) alternative configurations of the health care program. Again, the issue of whether funding will be available to support these priorities is moot.

BIBLIOGRAPHY

Aberle, D. F.
  1966 *The peyote religion among the Navajo.* Chicago: Aldine.
  1973 "Navajo." In D. M. Schneider and K. Gough, editors, *Matrilineal kinship.* Berkeley: University of California Press.
  1981 "A century of Navajo kinship change." *Canadian Journal of Anthropology* 2:21–36.
  1982 "The future of Navajo religion." In D. M. Brugge and C. J. Frisbie, editors, *Navajo religion and culture: Selected views.* Santa Fe: Museum of New Mexico Press.
Alfred, B. M.
  1970 "Blood pressure changes among Navajo migrants to an urban environment." *Canadian Review of Sociology* 7:189–200.
Beaglehole, R., C. E. Salmond, A. Hooper, J. Huntsman, J. M. Stanhope, J. C. Cassel, and I.A.M. Prior
  1977 "Blood pressure and social interaction in Tokelauan migrants in New Zealand." *Journal of Chronic Diseases* 30:803–812.
Beals, R.
  1953 "Acculturation." In A. L. Kroeber, editor, *Anthropology Today.* Chicago: University of Chicago Press.
Bengston, V. L.
  1979 "Ethnicity and aging: Problems and issues in current social science inquiry." In D. E. Gelfand and A. J. Kutzik, editors, *Ethnicity and aging.* New York: Springer Publishing Co.
Bergner, M., R. A. Bobbitt, S. Kressel, W. E. Pollard, B. S. Gilson, and J. R. Morris
  1976a "The sickness impact profile: Conceptual formulation and method-

ology for the development of a health status measure." *International Journal of Health Services* 6:393–415.

Bergner, M., R. A. Bobbitt, W. E. Pollard, D. M. Martin, and B. S. Gilson
1976b "The sickness impact profile: Validation of a health status measure." *Medical Care* 14:47–57.

Berkman, L. F.
1983 "The assessment of social networks and social support in the elderly." *Journal of the American Geriatric Society* 31:743–749.
1984 "Assessing the physical health effects of social networks and social support." *Annual Review of Public Health* 5:413–432.
1986 "Social networks, support, and health: Taking the next step forward." *American Journal of Epidemiology* 123:559–562.

Berkman, L. F., and S. L. Syme
1979 "Social networks, host resistance, and mortality: A nine-year follow-up study of Alameda County residents." *American Journal of Epidemiology* 109:186–204.

Bice, T. W., R. L. Eichhorn, and P. D. Fox
1972 "Socioeconomic status and use of physician services: A reconsideration." *Medical Care* 10:261–271.

Blazer, D.
1982 "Social support and mortality in an elderly community population." *American Journal of Epidemiology* 115:684–694.

Blazer, D., and C. Williams
1980 "Epidemiology of dysphoria and depression in an elderly population." *American Journal of Psychiatry* 137:439–444.

Block, M. R.
1979 "Exiled Americans: The plight of Indian aged in the United States." In D. E. Gelfand and A. J. Kutzik, editors, *Ethnicity and aging.* New York: Springer Publishing Co.

Blumer, H.
1971 "Social problems as collective behavior." *Social Problems* 18:298–306.

Boyce, W. T., C. Schaefer, H. R. Harrison, W.H.J. Haffner, M. Lewis, and A. L. Wright
1986 "Social and cultural factors in pregnancy complications among Navajo women." *American Journal of Epidemiology* 124:242–253.

Branch, L. G., and F. J. Fowler
1975 *The health care needs of the elderly and chronically disabled in Massachusetts.* Boston: Survey Research Program of the University of Massachusetts and the Joint Center for Urban Studies of MIT and Harvard University.

Branch, L. G., and A. M. Jette
1984 "Personal health practices and mortality among the elderly." *American Journal of Public Health* 74:1126–1129.

Branch, L. G., S. Katz, K. Kniepmann, and J. A. Papsidero
  1984 "A prospective study of functional status among community elders." *American Journal of Public Health* 74:266-268.
Broadhead, W. E., B. H. Kaplan, S. A. James, E. H. Wagner, V. J. Schoenbach, R. Grimson, S. Heyden, G. Tibblin, and S. H. Gehlbach
  1983 "The epidemiologic evidence for a relationship between social support and health." *American Journal of Epidemiology* 117:521-537.
Broudy, D. W., and P. A. May
  1983 "Demographic and epidemiologic transition among the Navajo Indians." *Social Biology* 30:1-16
Brown, G. W., M. Ni Bhrolchain, and T. O. Harris
  1975 "Social class and psychiatric disturbance among women in an urban population." *Sociology* 9:225-254.
Buschan, G.
  1910 *Illustrierte Volkerkunde.* 2 vols. Stuttgart: Strecker.
Callaway, D. G., J. E. Levy, and E. B. Henderson
  1976 *The effects of power production and strip mining on local Navajo populations.* Lake Powell Research Project Bulletin No. 22. Los Angeles: Institute of Geophysics and Planetary Physics, University of California.
Carr, B. A.
  1978 *Projection of Navajo male and female elderly through the year 2000.* Window Rock, Ariz.: Department on Aging, Navajo Tribe.
Carr, B. A., and E. S. Lee
  1978 "Navajo tribal mortality: A life table analysis of the leading causes of death." *Social Biology* 25:279-287.
Cassel, J.
  1974 "Hypertension and cardiovascular disease in migrants: A potential source of clues?" *International Journal of Epidemiology* 3:204-206.
  1976 "The contribution of the social environment to host resistance." *American Journal of Epidemiology* 104:107-123.
Cassel, J., R. Patrick, and D. Jenkins
  1960 "Epidemiological analysis of the health implication of culture change: A conceptual model." *Annals of the New York Academy of Science* 84:938-949.
Clark, M.
  1973 "Contributions of cultural anthropology to the study of the aged." In L. Nader and W. Maretzky, editors, *Cultural illness and health.* Anthropological Studies 9. Washington, D.C.: American Anthropological Association.
Coale, A. J., and E. E. Kisker
  1986 "Mortality crossovers: Reality or bad data?" *Population Studies* 40:389-401.

Cobb, S.
   1976   "Social support as a moderator of life stress." *Psychosomatic Medicine*
          38:300–314.
Collier, M. C.
   1951   "Local organization among the Navajo." Ph.D. diss. Department of
          Anthropology, University of Chicago.
Committee on Criteria
   1960   "Conference on methodology in epidemiological studies of cardio-
          vascular disease." *American Journal of Public Health* 50: No. 10, Sup-
          plement.
Comstock, G. W., and K. J. Helsing
   1976   "Symptoms of depression in two communities." *Psychological Med-
          icine* 6:551–563.
Cowgill, D. O.
   1972   "A theory of aging in cross-cultural perspective." In D. O. Cowgill
          and L. D. Holmes, editors, *Aging and Modernization*. New York:
          Appleton-Century-Crofts.
Craig, T. J., and P. A. Van Natta
   1983   "Disability and depressive symptoms in two communities." *Amer-
          ican Journal of Psychiatry* 140:598–601.
Crandell, D. L., and B. P. Dohrenwend
   1967   "Some relations among psychiatric symptoms, organic illness, and
          social class." *American Journal of Psychiatry* 123:1527–1538.
Department of Health Services
   1977   *Sickness impact profile.* Seattle: School of Public Health, University of
          Washington.
DeStefano, Frank, J. L. Coulehan, and M. K. Wiant
   1979   "Blood pressure survey on the Navajo Indian Reservation." *Amer-
          ican Journal of Epidemiology* 109:335–345.
DHIS. *See* Navajo Tribe. Department of Health Improvement Services.
Dressler, W. W., and L. W. Badger
   1985   "Epidemiology of depressive symptoms in Black communities."
          Journal of Nervous and Mental Disease. 173:212–220.
Dunkle, R. E.
   1983   "The effect of elders' household contribution on their depression."
          Journal of Gerontology 6:732–737.
Eaton, W. W., and L. G. Kessler
   1981   "Rates of symptoms of depression in a national sample." *American
          Journal of Epidemiology* 114:528–538.
Ensel, W. M.
   1982   "The role of age in the relationship of gender and marital status to
          depression." *Journal of Nervous and Mental Disease* 170:536–543.
Estes, C. L.
   1979   *The aging enterprise: A critical examination of social policies and services for
          the aged.* San Francisco: Jossey-Bass Publishers.

Estes, C. L., L. E. Gerard, J. S. Zones, and J. H. Swan
1984 *Political economy, health, and aging.* Boston: Little, Brown and Co.
Estes, C. L., and P. R. Lee
1985 "Social, political, and economic background of long term care policy." In C. Harrington, R. J. Newcomer, and C. Estes, editors, *Long term care of the elderly: Public policy issues.* Beverly Hills: Sage Publications.
Fabrega, H.
1974 "Problems implicit in the social and cultural study of depression." *Psychosomatic Medicine* 36:377–398.
Foner, N.
1984 "Age and social change." In D. I. Kertzer and J. Keith, editors, *Age and Anthropological Theory.* Ithaca, N.Y.: Cornell University Press.
Freed, S. A., and R. S. Freed
1971 "A technique for studying role behavior." *Ethnology* 9:107–121.
Freidson, E.
1971 *Profession of Medicine.* New York: Dodd, Mead.
Frerichs, R. R., C. S. Anesheusal, P. Yopenik, and V. A. Clark
1982 "Physical health and depression: An epidemiological survey." *Preventive Medicine* 11:639–646.
Fulmer, H. S., and R. W. Roberts
1963 "Coronary heart disease among the Navajo Indians." *Annals of Internal Medicine* 59:740–764.
Geertsen, R., R. L. Kane, M. R. Klauber, M. Rindflesh, and R. Gray
1975 "A re-examination of Suchman's views of social factors in health care utilization." *Journal of Health and Social Behavior* 16:226–237.
Gilson, B. S., J. S. Gilson, M. Bergner, R. A. Bobbitt, S. Kressel, W. E. Pollard, and M. Vesselago
1975 "The sickness impact profile: development of an outcome measure of health care." *American Journal of Public Health* 65:1304–1310.
Goodman, J. M.
1982 *The Navajo atlas: Environments, resources, people, and history of the Dine Bikeyah.* Norman: University of Oklahoma Press.
Goodwin, Grenville
1969 *The social organization of the western Apache.* 2d. ed. Tucson: University of Arizona Press.
Goody, J.
1983 *The development of the family and marriage in Europe.* Cambridge: Cambridge University Press.
Green, V. L.
1984 "Premature institutionalization among the rural elderly in Arizona." *Public Health Reports* 99:58–63.
Guillemin, J.
1980 "Federal policies and Indian politics." *Transaction* (May/June): 29–34.

Hajnal, J.
   1965   European marriage patterns in perspective. In D. V. Glass and
          D.E.C. Eversley, editors, *Population in history: Essays in historical de-
          mography.* London: Edward Arnold Publishers.
   1982   "Two kinds of preindustrial household formation system." *Popula-
          tion and Development Review* 8:449–494.
Harrington, C., R. J. Newcomer, and C. Estes
   1985   *Long term care of the elderly: Public policy issues.* Sage Library of Social
          Research, 157. Beverly Hills: Sage Publications.
Henderson, Eric B.
   1979   "Skilled and unskilled blue collar Navajo workers: Occupational
          diversity in an American Indian tribe." *Social Science Journal* 16:
          63–80.
   1982   "Kaibeto Plateau ceremonialists, 1860–1980." In D. M. Brugge and
          C. J. Frisbie, editors, *Navajo religion and culture: Selected views.* Sante
          Fe: Museum of New Mexico Press.
   1985   "Status and social change among the western Navajo." Ph.D. diss.
          Department of Anthropology. University of Arizona, Tucson.
Henderson, Eric B., and Jerrold E. Levy
   1975   *Survey of Navajo community studies, 1936–1974.* Lake Powell Research
          Project Bulletin 6. Los Angeles: Institute of Physics and Geophys-
          ics, University of California.
House, J. S., K. R. Landis, and D. Umberson
   1988   "Social relationships and health." *Science* 241:540–545.
House, J. S., C. Robbins, and H. L. Metzner
   1982   "The association of social relationships and activities with mortal-
          ity: Prospective evidence from the Tecumseh community health
          study." *American Journal of Epidemiology* 116:123–140.
Johnson, C., and L. Grant
   1985   *The nursing home in American society.* Baltimore: Johns Hopkins Uni-
          versity Press.
Johnston, D. F.
   1966   *An analysis of sources of information on the population of the Navajo.*
          Bureau of American Ethnology Bulletin 197, Washington, D.C.: U.S.
          Government Printing Office.
Joseph, J. G., I.A.M. Prior, C. E. Salmond, and D. Stanley
   1983   "Elevation of systolic and diastolic blood pressure associated with
          migration: The Tokelau Island migrant study." *Journal of Chronic
          Diseases* 36:507–516.
Kane, R. A., and R. L. Kane
   1981   *Assessing the elderly: A practical guide to measurement.* Lexington, Mass.:
          D. C. Heath and Co.
Katon, W., A. Kleinman, and G. Rosen
   1982   "Depression and somatization: Parts I and II." *American Journal of
          Medicine* 72:127–135, 241–247.

Katz, P. S., and P. May
1979   *Motor vehicle accidents on the Navajo Reservation, 1973–1975.* Window Rock, Ariz.: Navajo Health Authority.

Katz, S., and C. A. Akpom
1976   "A measure of primary sociobiological functions." *International Journal of Health Services* 6:493–508.

Katz, S., L. G. Branch, M. H. Branson, J. A. Papsidero, J. C. Beck, and D. S. Greer
1983   "Active life expectancy." *New England Journal of Medicine* 309:1218–1224.

Kelly, L. C.
1968   *The Navajo Indians and federal Indian policy.* Tucson: University of Arizona Press.

Kluckhohn, C.
1962   *Navajo witchcraft.* 2d ed. Boston: Beacon Press.

Kozarevic, D., B. Pirc, N. Vojvodic, T. R. Dawber, T. Gordon, and W. J. Zukel
1977   "The Yugoslavia cardiovascular disease study: 3. Death by cause and area." *International Journal of Epidemiology* 6:129–134.

Kunitz, S. J.
1977a "Economic variation on the Navajo Reservation." *Human Organization* 36:186–193.

1977b "Underdevelopment and social services on the Navajo Reservation." *Human Organization* 36:398–404.

1983   *Disease change and the role of medicine: The Navajo Experience.* Berkeley: University of California Press.

Kunitz, S. J., and J. E. Levy
1986   "The prevalence of hypertension among elderly Navajos: A test of the acculturative stress hypothesis." *Culture, Medicine, and Psychiatry* 10:97–121.

1988   "A prospective study of isolation and mortality in a cohort of elderly Navajo Indians." *Journal of Cross-Cultural Gerontology* 3:71–85.

Kunitz, S. J., and J. C. Slocumb
1976   "The changing sex ratio of the Navajo Tribe." *Social Biology* 23:33–44.

Kunitz, S. J., and M. Tsianco
1981   "Kinship dependence and contraceptive use in a sample of Navajo women." *Human Biology* 53:439–452.

Laslett, P.
1975   "Societal development and aging." In R. Binstock and E. Shanas, editors, *Handbook on aging and social sciences.* New York: Van Nostrand Reinhold Co.

Lebra, T.
1976   *Japanese patterns of behavior.* Honolulu: University of Hawaii Press.

Leighton, D. C., and C. Kluckhohn
1947   *Children of the people: The Navajo individual and his development.* Cambridge, Mass: Harvard University Press.

Levy, J. E.
    1962   "Community organization of the western Navajo." *American An-thropologist* 64:781–801.
    1965   "Navajo suicide." *Human Organization* 24:308–318.
    1967   "The older American Indian." In E. G. Youmans, editor, *Older rural Americans*. Lexington: University of Kentucky Press.
    1980   "Who benefits from energy resource development: The special case of the Navajo Indians." *Social Science Journal* 17:1–19.
    1983   "Traditional Navajo health beliefs and practices." In S. J. Kunitz, *Disease change and the role of medicine: The Navajo experience.*

Levy, J. E., and S. J. Kunitz
    1974   *Indian drinking: Navajo practices and Anglo-American theories.* New York: John Wiley and Sons.
    1981   "Economic and political factors inhibiting the use of basic research findings in Indian alcoholism programs." *Journal of Studies on Alcohol*, supplement 9, 60–72.

Levy, J. E., S. J. Kunitz, and M. Everett
    1969   "Navajo criminal homicide." *Southwestern Journal of Anthropology* 25:124–152.

Levy, J. E., R. Neutra, and D. Parker
    1987   *Hand trembling, frenzy witchcraft, and moth madness: A study of Navajo seizure disorders.* Tucson: University of Arizona Press.

Libecap, G. D., and R. N. Johnson
    1980   "Legislating commons: The Navajo tribal council and the Navajo range." *Economic Inquiry* 18:69–85.

Lin, N., and W. M. Ensel
    1984   "Depression-mobility and its social etiology: The role of life events and social support." *Journal of Health and Social Behavior* 25:176–188.

Lin, N., M. W. Woelfl, and S. C. Light
    1985   "The buffering effect of social support subsequent to an important life event." *Journal of Health and Social Behavior* 26:247–263.

Litwak, E.
    1985a   "Complementary roles for formal and informal support groups: A study of nursing homes and mortality rates." *Journal of Applied Behavioral Science* 21:407–425.
    1985b   *Helping the elderly: The complementary roles of informal networks and formal systems.* New York: Guilford Press.

McCall, N.
    1985   "Evaluation of the Arizona Health Care Cost Containment System." HCFA Contract. Menlo Park, Calif.: Stanford Research Institute International.

McKinlay, J. B.
    1973   "Social networks, lay consultation and help-seeking behavior." *Social Forces* 51:275–292.

Manson, S. M., J. H. Shore, and J. D. Bloom
  1985 "The depressive experience in American Indian communities: A challenge for psychiatric theory and diagnosis." In A. Kleinman and B. Good, editors, *Culture and depression: Studies in the anthropology and cross-cultural psychiatry of affect and disorder.* Berkeley: University of California Press.
Markides, K. S., and R. Machalek
  1984 "Selective survival, aging and society." *Archives of Gerontology and Geriatrics* 3:207-222.
Marmot, M. G.
  1980 "Affluence, urbanization and coronary heart disease." In E. J. Clegg and J. P. Garlick, editors, *Disease and urbanization.* London: Taylor and Francis.
Marsella, A. J.
  1978 "Thoughts on cross cultural studies in the epidemiology of depression." *Culture, Medicine and Psychiatry* 2:343-357.
  1980 "Depression experience and disorder across cultures." In H. C. Triandis and J. G. Draguns, editors, *Handbook of cross-cultural psychology,* vol. 6: *Psychopathology.* Boston: Allyn and Bacon.
May, P. A., and M. B. Smith
  1988 "Some Navajo Indian opinions about alcohol abuse and prohibition: A survey and recommendations for policy." *Journal of Studies on Alcohol* 49:324-334.
Mick, C.
  1983 *A profile of American Indian nursing homes.* Tucson: Long Term Care Gerontology Center, University of Arizona.
Montero, D.
  1979 "Disengagement and aging among the Issei." In D. C. Gelfand and A. J. Kutzick, editors, *Ethnicity and aging.* New York: Springer Publishing company.
Murdock, S. H., and D. F. Schwartz
  1978 "Family structure and the use of agency services: An examination of patterns among elderly Native Americans." *Gerontologist* 18: 475-481.
Murphy, E.
  1982 "Social origins of depression in old age." *British Journal of Psychiatry* 141:135-142.
Murrell, S. A., S. Himmelfarb, and K. Wright
  1983 "Prevalence of depression and its correlates in older adults." *American Journal of Epidemiology* 117:173-185.
Nam, C. B., N. L. Weatherby, and K. A. Ockay
  1978 "Causes of death which contribute to the mortality crossover effect." *Social Biology* 25:306-314.
Nass, Barbara
  1980 "Surveys of BIA social services for elderly People in the Navajo

Nation." Window Rock, Ariz.: Navajo Aging Services Department, Navajo Tribe.

National Indian Council on Aging (NICOA)

    1976   *The Indian elder: A forgotten American.* Final Report of the First National Indian Conference on Aging. Albuquerque: Adobe Press.

    1980a *The role of states in social welfare programs for Indians.* Albuquerque: National Indian Council on Aging.

    1980b *Major federal laws and programs affecting the Indian elderly.* Albuquerque: National Indian Council on Aging

    1981a *American Indian elderly: A national profile.* Albuquerque: National Indian Council on Aging.

    1981b *Indian elderly and entitlement programs: An accessing demonstration project.* Albuquerque: National Indian Council on Aging.

    1981c *Indian tribal nursing homes and state regulations.* Albuquerque: National Indian Council on Aging.

Navajo Health Systems Agency

    1981   Nursing home services. Navajo Master Health Plan, FY 1981–2. Window Rock, Ariz.: Navajo Nation.

Navajo Tribal Council on Aging (NTCOA)

    1981   "Nihi masani' doo nihicheii baa' akonohsin." Final Report. Sponsored by the Navajo Nation Council on Aging and the Navajo Aging Services Department. March 23–25, 1981, Tsaile, Navajo Nation, Arizona.

Navajo Tribe. Department of Health Improvement Services (DHIS)

    1980   An assessment of unmet home care needs. DHIS Home Health Projects. Window Rock, Ariz.: Navajo Tribe.

    1984   "Navajo Nation home health service grant application." Window Rock, Ariz.: Navajo Tribe.

Navajo Tribe. Information Service Department

    1978   "Navajo population estimates." Window Rock, Ariz.: Navajo Tribe.

Navajo Yearbook

    1958   The Navajo yearbook: Report no. 7. Edited by R. W. Young. Window Rock, Ariz.: Navajo Agency.

Navarro, V.

    1976   "The political and economic determinants of health and health care in rural America." *Inquiry* 13:111–121.

Newman, J. P.

    1984   "Sex differences in symptoms of depression: Clinical disorder or normal distress?" *Journal of Health and Social Behavior* 25:136–159.

NICOA. *See* National Indian Council on Aging

Nisbet, R.

    1966   *The sociological tradition.* New York: Basic Books.

Norris, F. H., and S. A. Murrell
    1984   "Protective function of resources related to life events, global stress, and depression in older adults." *Journal of Health and Social Behavior* 25:424–437.

NTCOA. *See* Navajo Tribal Council on Aging

Oliver, C.
    1981   *The discovery of humanity: An introduction to anthropology.* New York: Harper & Row.

Omran, A. R.
    1971   "The epidemiologic transition: A theory of the epidemiology of population change." *Milbank Memorial Fund Quarterly* 49:509–538.

Palmore, E. B., and K. Manton
    1974   "Modernization and status of the aged: International correlations." *Journal of Gerontology* 29:205–210.

Parman, D. L.
    1976   *The Navajos and the New Deal.* New Haven: Yale University Press.

Piers, G., and M. B. Singer
    1953   *Shame and guilt: A psychoanalytic study.* Springfield, Ill.: Charles C. Thomas.

Pollard, W. E., R. A. Bobbitt, M. Bergner, D. P. Martin, and B. S. Gilson
    1976   "The sickness impact profile: Reliability of a health status measure." *Medical Care* 14:146–155.

Pritzlaff Commission on Long Term Care
    1984   *Long term care in Arizona: Executive summary.* Phoenix: Flinn Foundation.

Radloff, L. S.
    1977   "The CES-D scale: A self report depression scale for research in general population." *Applied Psychological Measurement* 1:385–401.

Redfield, R., R. Linton, and M. J. Herskowitz
    1936   "Memorandum on the study of acculturation." *American Anthropologist* 38:149–152.

Reed, D., D. McGee, and K. Yano
    1984   "Psychosocial processes and general susceptibility to chronic disease." *American Journal of Epidemiology* 119:356–370.

Reno, P.
    1981   *Mother Earth, Father Sky, and economic development: Navajo resources and their use.* Albuquerque: University of New Mexico Press.

Roberts, R. E., and S. W. Vernon
    1982   "Depression in the community: Prevalence and treatment." *Archives of General Psychiatry* 39:1407–1409.

Robins, L. N., J. E. Helzer, J. Croughan, and K. Ratcliff
    1981   "The National Institute of Mental Health diagnostic interview schedule: Its history, characteristics and validity." *Archives of General Psychiatry* 38:381–389.

Robins, L. N., J. E. Helzer, J. Croughan, J.B.W. Williams, and R. L. Spitzer
  1981 "NIMH diagnostic interview schedule: Version III." Unpublished
        copy for circulation. Bethesda, Md.: National Institute of Mental
        Health.
Rogers, C. J., and T. E. Gallion
  1978 "Characteristics of elderly Pueblo Indians in New Mexico." *Geron-
        tologist* 18:482–487.
Salloway, J. C., and P. B. Dillon
  1973 "A comparison of family networks and friend networks in health
        care utilization." *Journal of Comparative Family Studies* 4:131–142.
Salmond, C. E., I.A.M. Prior, and A. F. Wessen
  1989 "Blood pressure patterns and migration: A 14-year cohort study of
        adult Tokelauans." *American Journal of Epidemiology* 130:37–52.
Schoenbach, V. J., B. H. Kaplan, L. Fredman, and D. G. Kleinbaum
  1986 "Social ties and mortality in Evans County, Georgia." *American
        Journal of Epidemiology* 123:577–591.
Simmons, L.
  1945 *The role of the aged in primitive society*. New Haven: Yale University
        Press.
Starr, P.
  1982 *The social transformation of American medicine*. New York: Basic Books.
Suchman, E. A.
  1964 "Sociomedical variations among ethnic groups." *American Journal of
        Sociology* 70:319–331.
  1965 "Social patterns of illness and medical care." *Journal of Health and
        Human Behavior* 6:2–16.
Suzman, R. M., D. J. Voorhees-Rosen, and D. H. Rosen
  1980 "The impact of North Sea oil development on mental and physical
        health: A longitudinal study of the consequences of an economic
        boom and rapid social change." Paper presented at the annual
        meeting of the American Sociological Association, New York.
Thoits, P. A.
  1982 "Conceptual, methodological, and theoretical problems in study-
        ing social support as a buffer against life stress." *Journal of Health
        and Social Behavior* 23:145–159.
Thurow, L. C.
  1985 "Medicine versus economics." *New England Journal of Medicine*
        313:611–614.
Timmreck, T. C., and A. Brown
  1984 *A survey on long term care and aging policy of the Navajo Tribal Council:
        Results and findings*. Tucson: Long Term Gerontology Center, Uni-
        versity of Arizona.
Uhlenhuth, E. H., R. S. Lipman, M. B. Balter, and M. Stern
  1974 "Symptom intensity and life stress in the city." *Archives of General
        Psychiatry* 31:759–764.

U.S. Bureau of the Census
 1982 "Census of population and housing, 1980: Summary tape file 1." Washington, D.C.: Superintendent of Documents.
U.S. Department of the Interior. Bureau of Indian Affairs (BIA)
 1972 Navajo population estimate. Window Rock, Ariz.: Navajo Area Office, Office of Information and Statistics.
U.S. Public Health Service (USPHS)
 1957 *Health services for American Indians.* U.S. Department of Health, Education, and Welfare, PHS Publication no. 531. Washington, D.C.: U.S. Government Printing Office.
 1978 *Facts of life and death.* U.S. Department of Health, Education, and Welfare, PHS Publication no. 79-1222. Washington, D.C.: U.S. Government Printing Office.
 1980 *Navajo population.* U.S. Public Health Service, Office of Program Planning and Statistics, Statistics Branch. Window Rock, Ariz: Navajo Area Indian Health Service.
 1983 *Nursing and related care homes as reported from the NMFI Survey.* Data from the National Health Survey, Series 14, No. 29. DHHS Publication 84-1824. Hyattsville, Md.: U.S. Department of Health and Human Services, National Center for Health Statistics.
University of Washington. Department of Health Services
 1977 *Sickness impact profile.* Seattle: School of Public Health, University of Washington.
Verbrugge, L. M.
 1985 "Gender and health: An update on hypotheses and evidence." *Journal of Health and Social Behavior* 26:156-182.
Vogt, E.
 1951 *Navajo veterans: A study of changing values.* Papers of the Peabody Museum of American Archeology and Ethnology, vol. 41, No. 1. Cambridge, Mass.
Wahrheit, G. J., C. E. Holzer, and J. J. Schwab
 1973 "An analysis of social class and racial differences in depressive symptomatology: A community study." *Journal of Health and Social Behavior* 14:291-295.
Waldo, D. R., and H. C. Lazenby
 1984 "Demographic characteristics and health care use and expenditures by the aged in the United States, 1977-1984. *Health Care Financing Review* 6:1-29.
Weatherby, N. L., C. B. Nam, and L. W. Isaac
 1983 "Development, inequality, health care, and mortality at the older ages: A cross-national analysis." *Demography* 20:27-43.
Weiss, I. K., C. L. Nagel, and M. K. Aronson
 1986 "Applicability of depression scales to the old, old person." *Journal of the American Psychiatric Society* 34:215-218.

Weissman, M. M., and G. L. Klerman
    1977   "Sex differences and the epidemiology of depression." *Archives of General Psychiatry* 34:98-112
    1978   The epidemiology of mental disorders: emerging trends. *Archives of General Psychiatry* 35:705-712.
Weissman, M. M., and J. K. Myers
    1979   "Depression in the elderly: Research directions in psychopathology, epidemiology and treatment." *Journal of Geriatric Psychiatry* 7:187-201.
    1980   "Depression in New Haven, 1975-76: An epidemiological study." *Yale Journal of Biology and Medicine* 53:117-126.
Welin, L., K. Svarsudd, S. Ander-Peciva, G. Tibblin, B. Tibblin, B. Larsson, and L. Wilhelmsen
    1985   "Prospective study of social influences on mortality." *Lancet*, April 20, 915-918.
Williams, G. C.
    1980   "Warriors no more: A study of the American Indian elderly." In C. Fry, editor, *Aging in culture and society*. New York: J. F. Bergin Publishers.
Wing, J. K., and P. Bebbington
    1982   "Epidemiology of depressive disorders in the community." *Journal of Affective Disorders* 4:331-345.
Wing, S., K. G. Manton, E. Stallard, C. G. Hames, and H. A. Tyroler
    1985   "The black/white mortality crossover: Investigation in a community-based study." *Journal of Gerontology* 40:78-84.
Wolinsky, F. D.
    1982   "Racial differences in illness behavior." *Journal of Community Health* 8:87-101.
Wood, J. J.
    1980   "Rural western Navajo household income strategies." *American Ethnologist* 7:493-503.
Zuckerman, D. M., S. V. Kasl, and A. M. Ostfeld
    1984   "Psychosocial predictors of mortality among the elderly poor." *American Journal of Epidemiology* 119:410-423.
Zung, W. W.
    1965   "A self rating depression scale." *Archives of General Psychiatry* 12: 63-70.

Index

Accidents, 95, 96, 107–9

Acculturation: assimilation, 74; cultural disintegration, 75; definition of, 74; indicators of, 75; of Navajos, 81–84, 89

Administration on Aging, Department of Health and Human Services, 115, 170

Adult Foster Care for Navajos, 135; in Crownpoint, 135; in Tuba City, 135

Advisory Council on Indian Health Care (Arizona), 170

Aging: changing context of, 13–27, 167; of Western industrial population, 1. *See also* Elderly

Aging, Department on. *See* Department on Aging

Aid to Families with Dependent Children, 18

Alcohol abuse. *See* Drinking

Apaches, Western, 3

Arizona Health Care Cost Containment System (AHCCCS), 117

Arizona Long Term Care System (ALTCS), 170, 171

Assimilation. *See* Acculturation

Begashie, 18, 24. *See also* Bridget

Black Mesa, 5; strip mining of, 7

Blood pressure. *See* Hypertension

Bridget (daughter of Begashie), 18, 22–26

Bureau of Indian Affairs, 113, 116

Cameron-Gray Mountain community, 42

Camps (Navajo extended families): 8–9, 41–52, 168–69; age distribution at, 44; characteristics of, 44; children in, 45–48, 66, 69; cooperation between, 19, 22; economy of, 20; education at, 44; income of, 20; marital status in, 45; matrilocal, 9, 41–42, 45; men in, 44–47; neolocal, 42, 43, 45, 47–48; number of people in, 66; patrilocal, 42, 45; women in, 44–47

ABOUT THE AUTHORS

STEPHEN J. KUNITZ received a medical degree from the University of Rochester and a Ph.D. in sociology from Yale University. He first worked on the Navajo Reservation as a physician in the U.S. Public Health Service in the mid-1960s. It was then that he became involved in research on the health conditions of American Indians. His first book, *Indian Drinking: Navajo Practices and Anglo-American Theories* (1974), written with Jerrold Levy, was begun at that time. He has also written *Disease Change and the Role of Medicine: The Navajo Experience* (1983). Professor Levy and he are currently engaged in a follow-up study of the people first interviewed in the 1960s for their study of alcohol use and abuse. In addition, Dr. Kunitz has written on the history of medicine as well as on historical demography. He is Associate Professor in the Department of Community and Preventive Medicine at the University of Rochester School of Medicine and Dentistry.

JERROLD E. LEVY received an M.A. in Oriental languages and literatures and a Ph.D. in anthropology from the University of Chicago. He first worked on the Navajo Reservation from 1959 to 1964, as an anthropologist with the Indian Health Service, and has been a professor of anthropology at the University of Arizona since 1972. In addition to work co-authored with Stephen Kunitz, he co-authored *Hand Trembling, Frenzy Witchcraft, and Moth Madness: A Study of Navajo Seizure Disorders* (1987) with Raymond Neutra and Dennis Parker. He has recently finished a book on the Hopi Indians.